S0-AHA-253

NOW AVAILABLE

The programs in this book are now available in source code on disk (5.25"; 360 KB) for your IBM PC (and most compatibles).

Order the program disk *today* priced £12.65/$26.22 (VAT inclusive) from your computer store, bookseller, or by using the order form below. Alternatively you can telephone your credit card order on (0243) 829121, Customer Service Department, John Wiley & Sons.

Ammeraal: Graphics Programming in Turbo C® —Program Disk

Please send me ...... copies of **Ammeraal: Graphics Programming in Turbo C®** —Program Disk at £12.65/$26.22 **(VAT inclusive)** each.

ISBN 0 471 92446 6

POSTAGE AND HANDLING FREE FOR CASH WITH ORDERS OR PAYMENT BY CREDIT CARD

☐ Remittance enclosed .... Allow approx. 14 days for delivery

☐ Please charge this order to my credit card (All orders subject to credit approval)

Delete as necessary:—AMERICAN EXPRESS, DINERS CLUB, BARCLAYCARD/VISA, ACCESS/MASTERCARD

CARD NUMBER   Expiration date...................

☐ Please send me an invoice for prepayment. A small postage and handling charge will be made.

Software purchased for professional purposes is generally recognized as tax deductible.

NAME/ADDRESS ....

....

....

OFFICIAL ORDER NUMBER .... SIGNATURE ....

If you have any queries about the compatibility of your hardware configuration, please contact:

Helen Ramsey
John Wiley & Sons Limited
Baffins Lane
Chichester
West Sussex
PO19 1UD
England

(0243) 770377

Affix
stamp
here

Customer Service Department
John Wiley & Sons Limited
Distribution Centre
Shripney Road
Bognor Regis
Sussex
PO22 9SA
England

*Graphics Programming
in Turbo C®*

Graphics Programming in Turbo C®

Leendert Ammeraal

Hogeschool Utrecht
The Netherlands

JOHN WILEY & SONS
Chichester · New York · Brisbane · Toronto · Singapore

Copyright © 1989 by John Wiley & Sons Ltd.
Baffins Lane, Chichester
West Sussex PO19 1UD, England

Reprinted February 1990

Other Wiley Editorial Offices

John Wiley & Sons, Inc., 605 Third Avenue,
New York, NY 10158-0012, USA

Jacaranda Wiley Ltd, G.P.O. Box 859, Brisbane,
Queensland 4001, Australia

John Wiley & Sons (Canada) Ltd, 22 Worcester Road,
Rexdale, Ontario M9W 1L1, Canada

John Wiley & Sons (SEA) Pte Ltd, 37 Jalan Pemimpin   05-04,
Block B, Union Industrial Building, Singapore 2057

British Library Cataloguing in Publication Data:

Ammeraal, L. (Leendert)
  Graphics programming in Turbo C.
  1. Microcomputer systems. Graphic displays.
  Programming
  I. Title
  006.6′6

ISBN 0 471 92439 3

Printed and bound in Great Britain by Courier International, Tiptree, Essex

Contents

Preface

The main subject of my previous book *Computer Graphics for the IBM PC* was the development of a set of useful graphics routines. When I wrote that book, C compilers did not offer any graphics facilities, so at the time there was a good reason for developing and publishing a graphics toolbox, based only on the ROM-BIOS routines, elementary output instructions, and direct access to graphics adapters. In only two years this situation has changed considerably. Turbo C (Version 2.0) from Borland International offers a very extensive set of graphics routines, and, as this compiler is very popular, attention has now shifted from developing basic graphics tools towards using such tools available in Turbo C. This is what the present book is about. As you read it, you may at first get the impression that most of the time I am using graphics C functions of my own instead of those from Borland. However, if you look more closely at the text of my graphics functions, you will see that they contain calls to the Turbo C graphics functions and depend wholly on them. I have neither replaced nor supplemented Borland's graphics library but rather *used* it. As a consequence, the wide range of graphics adapters supported by Turbo C also applies to the graphics routines developed in this book.

Anyone who uses Turbo C for graphics applications will feel a need for more examples than those included in the Turbo C Reference Manual. I have therefore used many (illustrated) examples, ranging from a simple triangle to a complete interactive draw program. Chapter 1 describes some fundamental Turbo C graphics functions, a user-coordinate system, and the way Turbo C graphics drivers can be converted to object files and linked. Chapter 2 deals with the aspect ratio, circles, arcs, and lines of any width. Chapter 3 shows how we can obtain graphics results that can be incorporated into text documents, as I did when writing this book. It demonstrates the use of Hewlett-Packard Graphic Language (HP-GL), especially in connection with desktop publishing, for which WordPerfect (Version 5.0) is used as an example. It also contains the final version of a proposed graphics toolbox, called GRASPTC. Chapter 4 may be of interest to those who want to write graphics programs for amusement or perhaps for artistic reasons. Finally, Chapter 5 discusses the Turbo C functions associated with viewports and stored images. It also shows how we can get input data from a mouse, especially for the development of a mouse-controlled draw program, SDRAW, the complete source text of which is included.

Except for an example on spheres in Section 2.6, this book does not deal with three-dimensional graphics applications; if that is what you are interested in, you may try my previous books *Programming Principles in Computer Graphics* and *Interactive 3D Computer Graphics*. I have omitted this and some other graphics subjects to prevent this book from overlapping my three previous graphics books. Finding new subjects and new examples was in fact easier than I had expected.

I should like to express my thanks to my student Nico de Vries, who wrote a useful interrupt routine with access to the keyboard buffer; my interrupt routine (in Section 2.5) that deals with Ctrl-Break interrupts is a modified version of his. I am also grateful to Nikita Andreiev from San Carlos, California, who pointed out to me that we should be able to draw 'fat' lines, as discussed in Section 2.8.

Leendert Ammeraal

Trademarks

Genius Mouse is a registered trademark of Kun Ying Enterprise Co. Ltd.
Hercules is a registered trademark of Hercules Corp.
HP and HP-GL are registered trademarks of Hewlett-Packard Company.
IBM PC is a registered trademark of International Business Machines Corp.
Turbo C is a registered trademark of Borland International.
Ventura Publisher is a registered trademark of Ventura Software Inc.
WordPerfect is a registered trademark of WordPerfect Corp.

CHAPTER 1

Pixels, Lines, and Text

1.1 INTRODUCTION

Like any C program, a Turbo C graphics program consists mainly of functions. As the best way of writing C functions has recently been changed, we will avoid any confusion on this point, and begin with a subject of interest to any C programmer who uses a modern C compiler.

In this book we will consistently use the modern ANSI style of writing function definitions and declarations. For example, instead of the function

```
square(x, y, h) float x, y, h;
{ move(x-h, y-h); draw(x+h, y-h); draw(x+h, y+h);
  draw(x-h, y+h); draw(x-h, h-h);
}
```

written in the original style of Kernighan and Ritchie, we will now write

```
void square(float x, float y, float h)
{ move(x-h, y-h); draw(x+h, y-h); draw(x+h, y+h);
  draw(x-h, y+h); draw(x-h, h-h);
}
```

which is in accordance with the ANSI standard. In the terminology of the Turbo C User's Guide, we will use the *classic* style no longer, but employ the *modern* style instead. The keyword *void* enables us to write a *declaration* of a function that does not return a value in a natural way, as, for example,

```
void square(float x, float y, float h);
```

whereas in the classic style it would have been necessary to use keyword *int* instead of *void*, which would have been somewhat unnatural. Such a declaration is also called a *function prototype*. (I assume you to be familiar with the distinction between a function *definition*, that is, the function itself, and a function *declaration*, which only gives information about any returned value and (in the modern style) about any parameters. If a function has no parameters, we use the keyword *void* for another purpose, namely as an empty parameter list, as, for example, in

```
int readadigit(void)
{ char ch;
  ch = getchar();
  return (isdigit(ch) ? ch - '0' : -1);
}
```

If we omit the keyword *void* in the first line of this function, Turbo C will regard the function as being written in the classic style. Then the number of parameters is left undefined. By including this keyword, however, we tell the compiler that *readadigit* has no parameters, so if by mistake we write one or more arguments in a call to this function we will have an error message.

We must not use functions before their declarations. (In this regard a function *definition* counts as a *declaration*, so if a function is used only after its definition we need no separate declaration of that function.) This rule of using only predeclared functions also applies to 'standard' functions, such as, for example, *printf*. Fortunately, for every Turbo C standard function there is a header file (with a name ending in .H) which contains a declaration of that function. Since any such a declaration is written in the modern style we can also call it a function prototype. Consider, for example, the following program:

```
#include <stdio.h>
main()
{ puts("Hello");
}
```

Though extremely simple, this program is very instructive. In the classic style, the first line could be omitted, because then the compiler would assume *puts* to return an *int*-value (which is indeed the case). In the modern style we will preferably include this line, because the file STDIO.H includes the function prototype

```
int puts(char *string);
```

which enables the compiler to check if in our call of *puts* there is exactly one argument of the correct type. For example, because of the first line of the above program, either of the following calls

```
puts("Hello", "Good Morning");
puts(123);
```

if written instead of *puts("Hello");* would cause the compiler to display an error message. If we had used these two lines without declaring the function *puts* (either directly or by means of including the file STDIO.H), then, instead of compile-time error messages, we would have had unpredictable results.

1.2 OUR FIRST GRAPHICS PROGRAM

We will now discuss a simple program that uses some important graphics functions available in Turbo C (Version 1.5 or higher). We will be using a rectangular coordinate system, the origin of which lies in the upper-left corner of the screen. Coordinates are integers, ranging from 0 to some maximum value that depends on the graphics adapter that is used. Let us use the variables $X\_\_max$ and $Y\_\_max$ for the maximum x- and y-values, respectively. (The double underscores in these variable names prevent any confusion with the names x_max and y_max that we will often use in this book for a different purpose.) Thus the situation is as shown in Fig. 1.1.

Fig. 1.1. Screen coordinates

Program TRIA draws the largest right-angled triangle that we can have on the screen; its right angle lies at the lower-left corner of the screen:

```
/* TRIA: A large right-angled triangle.
*/
#include <graphics.h>
#include <conio.h>

main()
{ int gdriver=DETECT, gmode, X_max, Y_max;
  initgraph(&gdriver, &gmode, "\\tc");

  X_max = getmaxx(); Y_max = getmaxy();
  moveto(0, Y_max);           /* Bottom left  */
  lineto(X_max, Y_max);       /* Bottom right */
  lineto(0, 0);               /* Top left     */
  lineto(0, Y_max);           /* Bottom left  */
  getch();
  closegraph();
}
```

If you wish to compile, link, and run this program successfully, there are two special points to note:

1 You must tell the linker to search the graphics library for the graphics functions, such as *initgraph*, that occur in this program. In Turbo C (Version 2.0), the simplest way of doing this (when using the integrated environment) is by selecting *Options*, then *Linker*, to switch the option *Graphics library* to the *on* state (instead of the default state *off*). Don't forget also to select *Save options*, so that the compiler will remember your choice next time.

   Alternatively, you can use a *project file*. In this simple case this method is less attractive, but with larger programs, split up into several modules, we use project files in any case, and we may as well include the name GRAPHICS.LIB in these files. Here this method would work as follows. If the file name of this program is TRIA.C, then there must be a project file, say, TRIA.PRJ, with the following contents:

   ```
   tria
   graphics.lib
   ```

   We select this project file by pressing Alt-P, Enter and the name TRIA (or, in full, TRIA.PRJ).

2 The driver for your graphics adapter must be either in the directory \TC of the current drive or in the current directory. After installing Turbo C (Version 2.0) on a hard disk in the normal way the former will be the

case, but you can check this by looking for files with names ending in .BGI (short for Borland Graphics Interface) in the directory \TC. Remember that the above program will load the graphics driver it needs at run time! In Section 1.7 we will discuss a more sophisticated way of including graphics drivers in our programs.

Program TRIA contains calls to some Turbo C graphics functions. The header file GRAPHICS.H contains the declarations of many such functions; at this stage we consider those listed below:

```
void far initgraph(int far *graphdriver,
                   int far *graphmode,
                   char far *pathtodriver);
int far getmaxx(void);
int far getmaxy(void);
void far moveto(int x, int y);
void far lineto(int x, int y);
void far line(int x1, int y1, int x2, int y2);
void far closegraph(void);
```

The above occurrences of the keyword *far* cause the compiler to use long pointer formats; if they had been omitted, then with the 'Small' memory model there would have been conflicting pointer formats. As you may know, you can choose a memory model by selecting *Options*, then *Compiler*, and, finally, *Memory model*. As I often deal with large programs with large data areas, I always use the *Huge* memory model, so in my programs pointer formats are long in any case. If everyone did this, the keyword *far* would be superfluous!

The first of the above functions, *initgraph*, switches the computer from *text mode* to *graphics mode*, which is necessary whenever we want to produce graphics output on the screen. This important function has three parameters, which, together with their corresponding arguments in our program TRIA, are listed below:

Parameter	Argument
graphdriver	*&gdriver*
graphmode	*&gmode*
pathtodriver	*"\\tc"*

If we use the value *DETECT* (defined as 0 in GRAPHICS.H) for *graphdriver*, then *initgraph* will find which graphics adapter is in use, and assign an integer code, the 'graphics drivers constant', corresponding to that adapter, to our variable *gdriver*. Also, a code for the highest resolution available for that adapter is assigned to the variable *gmode*, given by means of the second argument. Finally, the directory where the graphics driver, for example HERC.BGI, can be found is given in the form of a string (or, in general, by means of a pointer to a character). In our example, this directory is \tc. Remember that in a string we must write two successive backslashes (\\) if we actually want only one (\), because a single backslash would act as an 'escape character'. For example, \t is the C notation for the tab-character. If *initgraph* cannot find the required graphics driver in the directory specified by *pathtodriver* it searches for it in the current directory. Accordingly, we can write the empty sting "" or the null pointer *NULL* if we want *initgraph* to search only the current directory.

The opposite of *initgraph* is the function *closegraph*, a call of which can be found at the end of program TRIA. We use it to switch back to text mode.

The functions *getmaxx* and *getmaxy* return the greatest values of X and Y that we can use in the current graphics mode. These values are dependent on the graphics adapter we have. In our programs we will store them in the variables X_max and Y_max so that we can use them more than once without calling *getmaxx* and *getmaxy* each time we need them. We can call these two functions only after calling *initgraph*.

The actual drawing of the triangle is done by calls of *moveto* and *lineto*. Recall that the coordinates are in fact integers denoting pixel numbers. They count from 0 and start at the top-left corner of the screen. With *moveto(X, Y)* and *lineto(X, Y)* it is as if we move a pen from some *current position* to point (X, Y); in contrast to *moveto*, *lineto* draws a straight line between the current position and point (X, Y).

Instead of

```
moveto(x1, y1); lineto(x2, y2); lineto(x3, y3);
```

we can write

```
line(x1, y1, x2, y2);
line(x2, y2, x3, y3);
```

We see that using *line* is disadvantageous if connected line segments are to be drawn, for then we have to specify the coordinates of each joining point (such as $x2$ and $y2$) twice.

1.3 PIXELS AND COLORS

This section deals with the possible states of individual pixels. With a mono-chrome graphics adapter, such as HGA, each pixel of the screen is either dark or light; with other adapters, for example EGA, there is a range of real colors available. We distinguish between a foreground and a background color, for either of which we can choose one of the available colors. Let us use the term *color* also for the distinction between dark and light pixels. Therefore this discussion about 'colors' also applies to monochrome graphics.

We will be using some Turbo C functions that in GRAPHICS.H are declared as follows:

```
int far getmaxcolor(void);
void far setcolor(int color);
void far setbkcolor(int color);
int far getcolor(void);
int far getbkcolor(void);
void far putpixel(int x, int y, int pixelcolor);
int far getpixel(int x, int y);
```

(We have briefly discussed the keyword *far* in Section 1.2, so henceforward we will ignore it.)

The colors that are available are numbered

$0, 1, 2, ..., getmaxcolor()$

so we can use the function *getmaxcolor* to inquire about the highest color number. With HGA, *getmaxcolor* returns the value 1, which denotes 'light', the normal *foreground color*, and 0 denotes 'dark', the normal *background color*. Also with a color screen, such as EGA, we often use only two colors. We then need not bother about the numeric codes of the colors, since we can write, for example:

```
int foregrcolor, backgrcolor, colorsum;
...
foregrcolor = getcolor();   /* Foreground color */
backgrcolor = getbkcolor(); /* Background color */
colorsum = foregrcolor + backgrcolor;
```

Remember that *getcolor* and *setcolor* relate to the foreground and that *getbkcolor* and *setbkcolor* refer to the background color. Adding two color codes may seem a very odd thing to do, but we can use the value of *colorsum* to invert a pixel, as the following function shows:

```
void invertpixel(int X, int Y)
{ putpixel(X, Y, colorsum - getpixel(X, Y));
}
```

We can easily verify that the third argument of *putpixel* will be *foregrcolor* if the call to *getpixel* returns *backgrcolor*, and vice versa.

If we want to use any colors other than the default foreground and background colors (which is obviously not the case if we are using monochrome graphics), then we should have some idea of the available color codes themselves. As far as the value of *getmaxcolor()* allows us to do so, we can use the colors listed in the following table:

Numerical value	Symbolic constant	Foreground or background?
0	BLACK	Both
1	BLUE	Both
2	GREEN	Both
3	CYAN	Both
4	RED	Both
5	MAGENTA	Both
6	BROWN	Both
7	LIGHTGRAY	Both
8	DARKGRAY	Foreground
9	LIGHTBLUE	Foreground
10	LIGHTGREEN	Foreground
11	LIGHTCYAN	Foreground
12	LIGHTRED	Foreground
13	LIGHTMAGENTA	Foreground
14	YELLOW	Foreground
15	WHITE	Foreground

The above symbolic constants are defined in the header file GRAPHICS.H, so if, for example, we want the background color to be green, we can write

```
setbkcolor(GREEN);
```

instead of

```
setbkcolor(2);
```

1.4 THE XOR WRITE MODE

Inverting pixels, as we did when discussing *getpixel* and *putpixel*, is often referred to as 'writing in XOR mode'. The abbreviation XOR stands for the '*exclusive or*' operation, written in C as ^. Recall that with *int* variables x and m the operation

```
x ^= m
```

inverts those bits in x for which the corresponding bits in the 'mask' m are one-bits.

In interactive graphics programs we normally want to use some variable point on the screen, indicated by a so-called *locator* or *cursor*. Using a graphics input device, such as a mouse, we can then move that locator to the position we want to indicate for some reason or other. When moving the locator, it frequently passes through graphics results, which it must not permanently destroy. This can be accomplished simply by inverting the pixels involved. When moving the locator on the screen, we invert the pixels that form its shape, and for each point affected by the locator the inversion is done twice: first, when the locator arrives at a point and, second, when it leaves it. Obviously, by inverting a pixel twice its original state is restored. We will therefore really use the *invertpixel* function, discussed in the previous section.

Now that we know how to invert individual pixels we can, in principle, invert all pixels on a line by calling the function *invertpixel* for all pixels that approximate that line. In Turbo C 1.5 we had to do this, but, fortunately, Turbo C 2.0 comes with a new function, declared as

```
void far setwritemode(int mode);
```

For *mode* we can use the following constants:

COPY_PUT $(= 0)$
XOR_PUT $(= 1)$

The default write mode is *COPY_PUT*; in this mode lines are normally drawn, regardless of anything already on the screen. In the *XOR_PUT* write mode, however, the pixels on the lines to be drawn are actually inverted. Due to this new function *setwritemode*, we can also use the standard Turbo C functions *moveto*, *lineto*, and *line* in cases where the pixels on a line are to be inverted, whereas before Version 2.0, in such cases, we had to use our own versions of these three functions, based on our function *invertpixel*. Since the Turbo C functions to draw lines are very fast, we prefer them to versions of our own.

Program CRHAIRS demonstrates the function *setwritemode*. After drawing a rectangle with many lines in it, it calls this function to switch to the *XOR_PUT* write mode, and then draws a horizontal and a vertical line, as shown in Fig. 1.2. Such lines are called *crosshairs*; they denote their point of intersection, and enable us to compare that point with other points with the same x- or y-coordinate. The interesting point about program CRHAIRS is that by pressing the four arrow keys we can move either the vertical or the horizontal crosshair without destroying anything else on the screen.

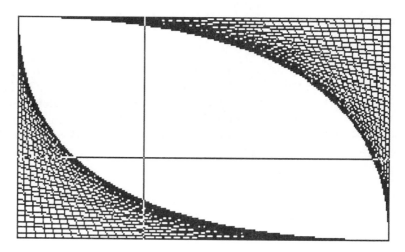

Fig. 1.2. Drawing with crosshairs

```
/* CRHAIRS: Crosshairs.
*/
#include <stdio.h>
#include <graphics.h>
#include <conio.h>
#define N 40
#define DX 15
#define DY 6

int Xmax, Ymax;

int round(float x)
 /*  The positive value x is rounded to the nearest integer */
{ return ((int)(x + 0.5));
}

void cross(int X, int Y)
{ static int Xcur=-1, Ycur=-1;
  if (X < 0) X = 0; if (X > Xmax) X = Xmax;
  if (Y < 0) Y = 0; if (Y > Ymax) Y = Ymax;
  if (X != Xcur)
  { if (Xcur >= 0) line(Xcur, 0, Xcur, Ymax);
                          /* Remove old line */
    line(X, 0, X, Ymax);    /* Draw new line   */
```

```
  }
  if (Y != Ycur)
  { if (Ycur >= 0) line(0, Ycur, Xmax, Ycur);
                            /* Remove old line  */
    line(0, Y, Xmax, Y);     /* Draw new line    */
  }
  Xcur = X; Ycur = Y;
}

main()
{ int gdriver=DETECT, gmode, i, OK, X, Y;
  char ch;
  float dX, dY;
  float redfact;
  /* We first draw some picture, in which later
     crosshairs will move without destroying it.
  */
  printf("Reduction factor (not greater than 1): ");
  scanf("%f", &redfact);
  printf("When in graphics mode, you can move the crosshairs "
         "by pressing any\nof the four arrow keys.\n");
  printf("\nPressing any other key will "
         "then cause the program to terminate.\n\n");
  printf("First, press any key to switch to the graphics mode ...");
  getch();
  initgraph(&gdriver, &gmode, "\\tc");
  Xmax = round(getmaxx()*redfact);
  Ymax = round(getmaxy()*redfact);
  dX = (float)Xmax / N; dY = (float)Ymax / N;
  for (i=0; i<=N; i++)
  { line(0, round(i * dY), round(i * dX), Ymax);
    line(Xmax, Ymax - round(i * dY), Xmax - round(i * dX), 0);
  }
  /* Crosshairs through the center of the screen:
  */
  setwritemode(XOR_PUT);
  X = Xmax/2; Y = Ymax/2;
  cross(X, Y);
  /* The crosshairs can now be moved:
  */
  OK = 1;
  while (OK && getch() == 0)
  { ch = getch();
    switch (ch)
    { case 72: cross(X, Y -= DY); break; /* Up    */
      case 75: cross(X -= DX, Y); break; /* Left  */
      case 77: cross(X += DX, Y); break; /* Right */
      case 80: cross(X, Y += DY); break; /* Down  */
```

```
      default: OK = 0;   /* Wrong key */
   }
 }
 closegraph();
}
```

This program contains some interesting aspects which deserve an explanation. As in most other interactive programs, we find a loop which begins with reading a character from the keyboard by calling *getch*. If this character is the null character (which we may denote by either 0 or '\0', not by '0') then a special key has been pressed, and the next character is immediately available. Among those special keys we are especially interested in the arrow keys, which have the following codes:

↑   0, 72
←   0, 75
→   0, 77
↓   0, 80

In each of these four cases either X or Y is updated and the function *cross* is called. Since only one arrow key can be pressed at a time, we have to move either the horizontal or the vertical crosshair. We detect which case applies by comparing the new X and Y values with the current values, *Xcur* and *Ycur*. These variables are 'static'; they will therefore keep their values between two calls of the function *cross*. As they have -1 as their initial values, they differ from both X and Y the first time *cross* is called, and therefore both crosshairs are drawn. Another special aspect of the first call is that in this case there are no old crosshairs to be erased, hence the two innermost if-clauses in this function.

1.5 USER COORDINATES

In graphics programs we usually have to solve some more or less difficult problems that are inherent to the applications themselves, and it would be most unfortunate if at the same time we had to bother about other difficulties arising from the hardware and basic software that we are using. One such problem is presented by the coordinate system we have been using. In many cases, especially if mathematical computations are involved, we prefer real numbers to integers. Besides, a y-axis pointing upward would be more conventional and therefore more convenient. We will therefore establish such a more convenient coordinate system, with the origin lying in the lower-left corner of the screen and with adapter-independent coordinates, which are real numbers. Let us divide the x-

axis on the screen into ten units, and write x_max for the largest x value. We also write y_max for the largest y value in our new coordinate system. Thus we have:

$$0 \le x \le x\_max$$
$$0 \le y \le y\_max$$
$(x = 0, y = 0$ in the lower-left corner)

We will sometimes call the new units 'inches', although for most monitors our new unit is actually somewhat less than an inch. After choosing $x\_max = 10$, we are now not completely free to select the value for y_max. Since the height of a computer screen is normally less than its width, y_max must be less than 10. In my previous graphics books I used the value 7.0 for this constant, but now that we are using Turbo C graphics we have to be very careful. This is because Turbo C comes with functions for circles and arcs, and these have their own method of dealing with the problem of using a correction factor for horizontal and vertical dimensions. We will discuss this subject (the *aspect ratio*) in Section 2.1. Let us now simply use $y\_max = 7.0$, bearing in mind that this value will change a little in Chapter 2. We can then use the following module, in which also the function *invertpixel* (discussed in Section 1.3) has been included:

```
/* GRASPTCO: Graphics System for Programming in Turbo C
             (Preliminary version)
*/
#include <graphics.h>
#include <conio.h>
int X__max, Y__max, foregrcolor, backgrcolor, colorsum;
float x_max=10.0, y_max=7.0, horfact, vertfact;

void initgr(void)
{ int gdriver=DETECT, gmode;
  initgraph(&gdriver, &gmode, "\\tc");
  foregrcolor = getcolor(); backgrcolor = getbkcolor();
  colorsum = foregrcolor + backgrcolor;
  X__max = getmaxx(); Y__max = getmaxy();
  horfact = X__max/x_max; vertfact = Y__max/y_max;
}

int IX(float x)
{ return (int) (x * horfact + 0.5);
}

int IY(float y)
{ return (int) Y__max - (int)(y * vertfact + 0.5);
}

void move(float x, float y)
/* User-coordinate version of 'moveto' */
```

```
{ moveto(IX(x), IY(y));
}

void draw(float x, float y)
/* User-coordinate version of 'lineto' */
{ lineto(IX(x), IY(y));
}

void line_uc(float x1, float y1, float x2, float y2)
/* User-coordinate version of 'line' */
{ line(IX(x1), IY(y1), IX(x2), IY(y2));
}

void endgr(void)
{ getch(); closegraph();
}

void invertpixel(int X, int Y)
{ putpixel(X, Y, colorsum - getpixel(X, Y));
}
```

With this module graphics programming will be much easier than it was in the
preceding sections. We can write many interesting graphics programs in which
occur no graphics function calls other than those below:

$initgr()$;   Initialize; switch to the graphics mode.

$move(x, y)$;   Move a fictitious pen to point (x, y), which becomes the '*current
position*'. The origin O lies in the bottom-left corner, and we have
$0 \leq x \leq 10$, $0 \leq y \leq 7$.

$draw(x, y)$;   Draw a line from the current position to point (x, y), which
becomes the new current position.

$endgr()$;   Wait until a key is pressed; then switch back to the text mode.

As we have seen in Section 1.1, we should declare every function before it is
used. We will therefore use the following *header file* of our own:

```
/* GRASPTCO.H: Header file, to be used in any module that uses the
               functions defined in GRASPTCO.
*/
#include <graphics.h>
extern int X__max, Y__max, foregrcolor, backgrcolor, colorsum;
extern float x_max, y_max, horfact, vertfact;

void initgr(void);
int IX(float x);
int IY(float y);
```

```
void move(float x, float y);
void draw(float x, float y);
void line_uc(float x, float y);
void endgr(void);
void invertpixel(int X, int Y);
```

In any program that uses our new functions we should use the line

```
#include "grasptc0.h"
```

to include the above header file.

We will normally not use the constants 10 and 7 in our programs, but rather x_max and y_max. Since these two variables are declared in the above header file we need not declare them ourselves.

Instead of program TRIA, listed in Section 1.2, we can now write:

```
/* TRIA1: This program draws a large triangle.
          (After compilation it is to be linked together
           with GRASPTC0.)
*/
#include "grasptc0.h"

main()
{ initgr();
  move(0.0, 0.0);      /* Lower left  */
  draw(x_max, 0.0);    /* Lower right */
  draw(0.0, y_max);    /* Upper left  */
  draw(0.0, 0.0);      /* Lower left  */
  endgr();
}
```

We must now not forget to link the module GRASPTC0 together with this main program, and we therefore now use a project file whose contents are:

```
tria1
grasptc0
graphics.lib
```

(You may omit the last line if you have instructed your compiler always to search the graphics library, as is possible with Turbo C Version 2.0.)

The four functions *initgr*, *move*, *draw*, and *endgr* are much easier to use than the 'standard' functions *initgraph*, *moveto*, *lineto*, and *closegraph*. As the above files

GRASPTC0.C and GRASPTC0.H show, the functions IX, IY, $line\_uc$, $invertpixel$ are also available for use in application programs, and the same applies to the global variables $X\_\_max$, $Y\_\_max$, x_max, y_max, $horfact$, $vertfact$, $foregrcolor$, $backgrcolor$, $colorsum$. We will see that they may sometimes be useful. Note that the maximum pixel coordinates $X\_\_max$ and $Y\_\_max$ depend on the graphics adapter we have, and it is helpful that after a call of $initgr()$ their correct values are immediately available. As for the maximum screen coordinates x_max and y_max, it is possible to give them values other than their default values 10.0 and 7.0, so if you wish, you can use a different unit of length, such as a millimeter. However, I would advise you not to do this until you have read Section 2.1. Remember, GRASPTC0 is only a preliminary version of GRASPTC, listed at the end of Chapter 3.

1.6 TEXT AND FONTS IN GRAPHICS MODE

Very often we want graphics output to contain pieces of text. Turbo C comes with two functions to accomplish this and they are declared in GRAPHICS.H as follows:

```
void far outtext(char far *textstring);
void far outtextxy(int x, int y, char far *textstring);
```

These differ in that $outtextxy$ is explicitly given the start point x, y (in pixel coordinates), whereas $outtext$ uses the current position as the start point. Normally (that is, without using $settextjustify$), the 'start point' is the upper-left corner of the first character.

In $text\ mode$, the shape of characters on the screen is determined by a piece of hardware called $character\ generator$, so there we cannot change these shapes. Incidentally, the technical term for character shapes is $font$. In $graphics\ mode$, on the other hand, characters simply consist of collections of dots; here every font that we desire can, in principle, be realized by means of software. As we will see shortly, several fonts and many sizes are available in Turbo C, but, for the time being, let us use the 'default' font and size; this means that each character is displayed in a rectangle of 8×8 pixels. When displaying text in the graphics mode there are no such facilities as automatically going to the beginning of the next line when a line is full, so we have to check whether the text we want to display fits within the screen boundaries. In doing this we must be careful not to confuse numbers of characters with numbers of pixels. Fortunately, Turbo C offers help in the form of two functions, declared in GRAPHICS.H as follows:

```
int far textwidth(char far *textstring);
int far textheight(char far *textstring);
```

These return the numbers of pixels that the text given by *textstring* will take in the horizontal and vertical directions, respectively. (This works correctly not only for the default character shape but also for other fonts and sizes.) For example, with X_max and Y_max as the maximum values of X and Y, we can display the text "*ABC*" in the extreme lower-right corner of the screen as follows:

```
outtextxy(X__max + 1 - textwidth("ABC"),
          Y__max + 1 - textheight("ABC"), "ABC");
```

If, for example, you are using the Hercules Graphics Adapter, the first and the second arguments in this call are

$$719 + 1 - 3 \times 8 = 696 \text{ and}$$
$$347 + 1 - 8 = 340,$$

respectively.

If only one font and size is not sufficient for our applications, we can use the following Turbo C function:

```
void far settextstyle(int font, int direction, int charsize);
```

(In fact, this is how this function is declared in GRAPHICS.H; as all graphics Turbo C functions are declared in this header file, I will henceforward not always mention this.)

The first argument, *font*, can be one of the integer values 0, 1, 2, 3, 4, with the following meaning:

Value	Symbolic constant
0	DEFAULT_FONT
1	TRIPLEX_FONT
2	SMALL_FONT
3	SANS_SERIF_FONT
4	GOTHIC_FONT

(Like functions, Turbo C symbolic constants for graphics are declared in GRAPHICS.H.) If we don't call *settextstyle* at all, the default font (with *font* = *DEFAULT_FONT*) is taken. This is 'bit mapped': it essentially consists of a bit pattern, not of line segments. The other fonts are *stroked*, which means that they are really drawn as line segments.

As values for the second argument, *direction*, we have:

Value	Symbolic constant
0	HORIZ_DIR
1	VERT_DIR

The default value is *HORIZ_DIR*. If we use *VERT_DIR*, text will be written in the vertical direction, as if normal text is rotated through 90° counterclockwise.

As you will expect, the third argument, *charsize*, determines the character size. By using the values 1, 2, ... 10 we can control the size of the characters: the greater the value of *charsize*, the larger the characters. With *charsize* = i ($1 \le i \le 10$), the bit-mapped characters will fit in a $8i \times 8i$ pixel rectangle on the screen. If we are using stroked fonts (that is, a font other than the default font), we have an even much finer control over the character size. We then have to use the value 0 for *charsize*, the third argument of *settextstyle*. In GRAPHICS.H the symbolic constant *USER_CHAR_SIZE* is defined, which we may use instead of 0. After this, we can use *setusercharsize*, declared as

```
void far setusercharsize(int multx, int divx, int multy, int divy);
```

The parameters *multx, divx, multy, divy* are used to scale the width and the height of the (stroked) characters: the default width is scaled by *multx* : *divx* and the default height by *multy* : *divy*. For example, to make text three times as wide and 2.5 times as high as the default we can use

multx = 3   *divx* = 1
multy = 5   *divy* = 2

So far, we have used the upper-left corner of the first character as the point that we supply to locate the string to be displayed. In general, we can use the function declared as

```
void far settextjustify(int horiz, int vert);
```

where both arguments can have the values 0, 1, 2, for which you may use the following symbolic constants:

Value	Symbolic constant
0	LEFT_TEXT, BOTTOM_TEXT
1	CENTER_TEXT
2	RIGHT_TEXT, TOP_TEXT

For example, program FONTDEMO displays the text

```
Turbo C
```

vertically (in triplex font), and the names of all five available fonts horizontally, each in its own font. If we link its object code together with GRASPTC0.OBJ we obtain the output shown in Fig. 1.3.

```c
/* FONTDEMO: Demonstration of Turbo C fonts
*/

#include "grasptc.h"

main()
{ int dY, XC;
  initgr();
  settextjustify(CENTER_TEXT, CENTER_TEXT);
  settextstyle(TRIPLEX_FONT, VERT_DIR, 3);
  outtextxy(160, Y__max/2, "Turbo C");

  XC = (X__max - 30)/2; dY = Y__max/8;

  settextstyle(DEFAULT_FONT, HORIZ_DIR, 4);
  outtextxy(XC, dY, "Default font");

  settextstyle(TRIPLEX_FONT, HORIZ_DIR, 4);
  outtextxy(XC, 2 * dY, "Triplex font");

  settextstyle(SMALL_FONT, HORIZ_DIR, 4);
  outtextxy(XC, 3 * dY, "Small font");

  settextstyle(SANS_SERIF_FONT, HORIZ_DIR, 4);
  outtextxy(XC, 4 * dY, "Sansserif font");

  settextstyle(GOTHIC_FONT, HORIZ_DIR, 4);
  outtextxy(XC, 5 * dY, "Gothic font");

  endgr();
}
```

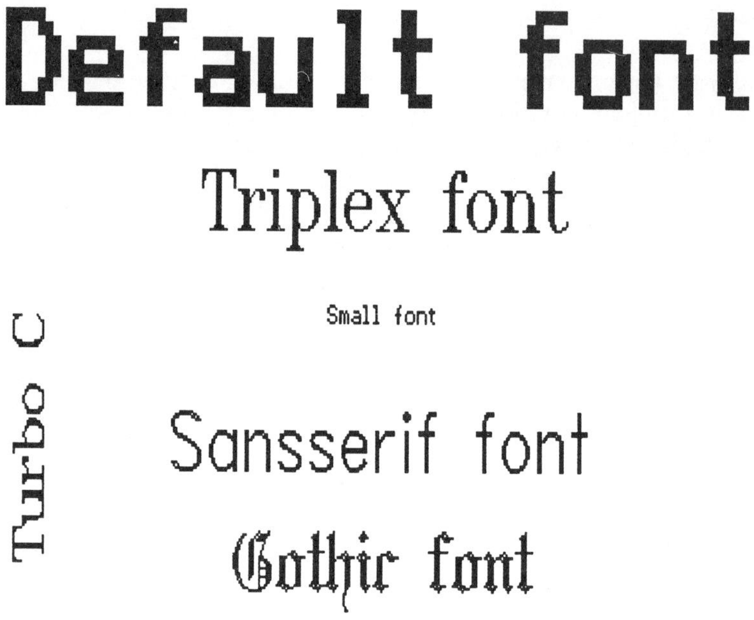

Fig. 1.3. Turbo C fonts

1.7 COMPILING AND LINKING GRAPHICS DRIVERS

Our module GRASPTC0, listed in Section 1.5, is far from complete. There are many useful graphics functions that we will be discussing in the remaining chapters, and once we are convinced of their usefulness we will want to include them in our graphics module. It is, after all, much more convenient to have a more or less complete module that has already been compiled and which needs only to be linked in than to search this book for those functions that your particular application needs. You can find the module GRASPTC at the end of Chapter 3. It contains the functions we have been discussing and many others. For some functions, we begin with simple versions, and replace them later with improved ones, which have the same names as the original versions. Dealing with several versions of some function will not be confusing, provided that we always bear in mind that the final version can be found in Chapter 3.

Besides extending the graphics functions themselves, we also have to improve the use of GRASPTC0 in quite a different way. Recall that in Section 1.2 we discussed the necessity for a graphics driver, such as, for example, HERC.BGI, to be available either in some fixed directory, say, \TC or in the current one. This seems to be only an insignificant complication, like so many others. After all, when compiling and linking, we have to be careful with header files and libraries, and with some programs we must pay attention to the memory model, so thinking about graphics drivers would make life no more complicated than it already is. However, we should distinguish between *programmers* and *users*. Although one might argue that programmers are in fact users of compilers and other systems software, we will adopt the conventional view that programmers write programs for users. It is the programmers' task to make life easy for users of their software, even if this makes their programs and development methods more complex. Applied to Turbo C graphics, this means that we want our executable programs (that is, our .EXE files) to be complete in the sense that their correct working should not depend on the availability of any separate graphics driver. Fortunately, Turbo C offers us the tools to accomplish this. There is a conversion utility for graphics drivers and fonts, called BGIOBJ, which converts drivers into object files. (Recall that BGI stands for Borland Graphics Interface.) There are six graphics driver files, namely, CGA.BGI, EGAVGA.BGI, HERC.BGI, ATT.BGI, PC3270.BGI, and IBM8514.BGI. Instead of using all six of them, let us, for example, restrict ourselves to the first three. Also, we will include only the first three of the following four available fonts files TRIP.CHR (triplex font), LITT.CHR (small font), SANS.CHR (sansserif font), and GOTH.CHR (gothic font). Using BGIOBJ is not really difficult. If the .BGI files are in our directory \TC, and the standard .OBJ and .LIB files are in \TC\LIB, then we can type:

```
cd \tc
bgiobj /F cga
bgiobj /F egavga
bgiobj /F herc
bgiobj /F trip
bgiobj /F litt
bgiobj /F sans
```

This will produce the files CGAF.OBJ, EGAVGAF.OBJ, HERCF.OBJ, TRIPF.OBJ, LITTF.OBJ, and SANSF.OBJ. We now move these from the directory \TC to the directory \TC\LIB, so we type

```
copy cgaf.obj \tc\lib
del cgaf.obj
```

followed by similar lines for the other five .OBJ files.

The next step consists of adding the six   .OBJ-files to the library GRAPHICS.LIB, which can be done as follows:

```
cd \tc\lib
tlib graphics +cgaf +egavgaf +hercf +tripf +littf +sansf
```

All this is done only once. After this, we can 'register' these files in our graphics programs, which means that we inform the graphics system of the presence of those files. We must do this *before* calling *initgraph*, for example, as follows:

```
registerfarbgidriver(CGA_driver_far);
registerfarbgidriver(EGAVGA_driver_far);
registerfarbgidriver(Herc_driver_far);
registerfarbgifont(triplex_font_far);
registerfarbgifont(small_font_far);
registerfarbgifont(sansserif_font_far);
initgraph(&gdriver, &gmode, "\\tc");
/* Pathname \tc will normally
   not be needed!
*/
if (graphresult())
{ printf("\nGraphics driver not available.\n");
  exit(1);
}
```

(Note the spelling of the symbolic names used as arguments of *registerfarbgidriver* and *registerfarbgifont*. If you need those for the drivers and the font we have not used, you should use: *ATT_driver_far, PC3270_driver_far, IBM8514_driver_far, gothic_font_far*.)

If our machine has one of the graphics adapters CGA, EGA, VGA, HGA, and we have extended our graphics library GRAPHICS.LIB in the way described above, then the pathname given as the third argument of *initgraph* is superfluous, so we might as well have written the empty string "". However, it may be a good idea to use a real pathname here, as shown above, in case the program is run on a machine with a different graphics adapter whose driver can be found by means of this pathname (or in the current directory).

If neither way is successful, the function *graphresult* will return a non-zero value, so that we can give an error message and stop program execution.

Normally, due to our use of the conversion utility BGIOBJ, the graphics drivers will be loaded as object files by the linker, instead of them being loaded as .BGI-files during program execution. In this way executable programs are complete entities. They include all graphics information, so that users of these programs need not worry about any graphics drivers. The programs will also run slightly faster, because during the execution of *initgraph* no graphics driver will be loaded from disk.

Linking graphics drivers and fonts, as we have just been doing, has one drawback: it makes the executable programs (.EXE files) considerably larger than they are with drivers and font loaded only at run time. You can therefore omit some of the lines

```
registerfarbgi...
```

in GRASPTC if you know that the driver or font mentioned in those lines will not be used. The executable program will then be much smaller. On the other hand, you can insert such lines for the drivers ATT, PC3270, IBM8514, and for the Gothic font, if you need these. If you run program FONTDEMO of Section 1.6 with my version of GRASPTC, then the file GOTH.CHR must be available, either in \TC, mentioned in the call to *initgraph* (see Section 1.6) or in the current directory, because I did not include this rather unusual font in GRASPTC.

CHAPTER 2

Circles, Arcs, and Polygons

2.1 ASPECT RATIO

Computations with integers are much faster than those with floating-point numbers, but the latter are often more convenient because they are more directly related to our applications. As in Section 1.5, we will write some convenient graphics functions that use floating-point arithmetic; we can regard these as an interface between what Turbo C offers and what we, as users, want. Thus, rather than bypassing the Turbo C graphics facilities, we will really use them, although in most cases in an indirect way.

In many graphics applications we want horizontal and vertical dimensions to be correct in relation to each other, so that shape is preserved. For example, a square must be drawn with four equal sides. Due to the nature of video display hardware, special procedures are required to achieve this. In this chapter, we will be dealing only with output on the computer screen. We will discuss the same problem with regard to the final document in Chapter 3, Section 3.3.

In general, the pixels of the computer screen are not squares. The distance between two adjacent pixels in a (vertical) column is greater than that between two adjacent pixels on a horizontal line, so we may regard each pixel as a rectangle whose height is greater than its width. Actually we should say 'greater than or equal to' rather than 'greater than', because with VGA, resolution 640×480, the pixels are squares. We will ignore this special case for a moment to make our discussion simpler. Our functions, however, will be quite general with regard to graphics adapters and will also be applicable to VGA.

It will be clear that the *aspect ratio*, that is, the ratio between the width and the height of a pixel, should be known if, for example, we want a circle to be drawn as a real circle, not as an ellipse. Turbo C offers a built-in function to obtain the aspect ratio, and, surprisingly, we can deal with this ratio in a very efficient way, without using floating-point variables. In order to express the height h and the width w in integers without sacrificing much numerical accuracy, we have to

25

use a very small unit of length. In Turbo C this unit is one ten-thousandth part of the height of a pixel; in other words, each pixel is 10 000 units high. Let us use the term *mini-units* for this new unit. All we now want to know is the width of a pixel, expressed in mini-units. We obtain this by writing

```
getaspectratio(&w, &h);
```

where w and h are integer variables, denoting the width and the height of a pixel expressed in mini-units. Thus, after this call, we have

$$h = 10000$$
$$w < 10000 \qquad \text{(except for VGA, where } w = 10000\text{)}$$

and our aspect ratio is $w : h$. Remember that our mini-units, just like inches or millimeters, always have a fixed length, regardless of the direction in which we measure them. This might seem obvious, but recall that it does not apply to numbers of pixels, although these numbers are often used as units of length. Consider, for example, a square with a horizontal side. Expressed in mini-units its height is equal to its width, but expressed in pixels it is not.

Program SQUARE1 uses our new concepts to draw a large square. Its height H (expressed in pixels) will be the height of the screen, so we write

```
H = getmaxy();
```

With h and w as defined above, we know that this height corresponds to Hh mini-units, so that the width of the square must also be Hh mini-units, which corresponds to Hh/w pixels. Program SQUARE1 uses this principle:

```
/* SQUARE1:
   Application of getaspectratio to the sides of
   a square. The square to be drawn should be as
   large as possible and there should be equal
   margins to its left and right.
*/

#include "grasptc.h"

main()
{ int w, h, W, H, margin;
  long len;
  initgr();
  getaspectratio(&w, &h);
  /* Width and height of pixel, in mini-units   */
  H = getmaxy();
```

```
      /* Height of square, in pixels             */
      len = (long)H * h;
      /* Length of its sides, in mini-units      */
      W = (int)(len/w);
      /* Width of square, in pixels              */
      margin = (getmaxx() - W)/2;
      /* Width of left and right margins, in pixels */
      moveto(margin, 0);
      lineto(margin + W, 0);
      lineto(margin + W, H);
      lineto(margin, H);
      lineto(margin, 0);
      endgr();
    }
```

Although I have tried to explain the Turbo C function *getaspectratio* as clearly as possible, it would not be surprising if you think the method of program SQUARE1 rather complicated. In Section 1.5 we have introduced user coordinates x and y, satisfying

$$0 \le x \le x\_max = 10.0$$
$$0 \le y \le y\_max = 7.0$$

(in which we should change the value 7.0, as we shall see shortly). Using these user coordinates, we can write program SQUARE2, which is much simpler than SQUARE1.

```
   /* SQUARE2: This program draws the same square as
                does program SQUARE1.
   */
   #include "grasptc.h"

   main()
   { float margin, a;
     initgr();
     a = y_max;         /* The length of a side */
     margin = 0.5 * (x_max - a);
     move(margin, 0.0);
     draw(margin + a, 0.0);
     draw(margin + a, a);
     draw(margin, a);
     draw(margin, 0.0);
     endgr();
   }
```

Unfortunately, if we use SQUARE2 in combination with module GRASPTC0, listed in Section 1.5, the resulting square is not identical to that drawn by

SQUARE1. This is so because program SQUARE2 does not use the aspect ratio returned by *getaspectratio*, while program SQUARE1 does. In the next section we will discuss some Turbo C functions for circles and arcs, which also use that aspect ratio, and for reasons of consistency, we want program SQUARE2 to do the same. After all, we must be able to draw a square with an inscribed circle. Fortunately, we need not change that program to switch to the required aspect ratio. Instead, we can modify the module GRASPTC0 in such a way that the value y_max depends on the aspect ratio $w : h$, obtained by the call *getaspectratio(&w, &h)*.

On the computer screen we have $X\_\_max + 1$ pixels on a horizontal line. Regarding these as points that lie some fixed distance apart, we see that there are $X\_\_max$ such small distances, which are the Turbo C units of length in the horizontal direction. Each of these units is equal to what we sometimes call the 'width of a pixel', and, as we have seen at the beginning of this section, that width is equal to w 'mini-units'. Thus the width of the screen is $X\_\_max \times w$ mini-units. Analogously, the height of the screen is equal to $Y\_\_max \times h$ mini-units. As mini-units are direction independent, we have

screen height : screen width $= (Y\_\_max \times h) : (X\_\_max \times w)$

Our user coordinates must also be direction independent, so y_max must be chosen such that $y\_max : x\_max$ is also equal to this ratio (which, incidentally, should not be confused with the aspect ratio). Thus we have

$y\_max : x\_max = (Y\_\_max \times h) : (X\_\_max \times w),$

which explains how y_max is computed in the following function:

```
void boundaries_uc(void)
{ int w, h;
  getaspectratio(&w, &h);
  y_max = x_max * (float)Y__max*h/((float)X__max*w);
  horfact = X__max/x_max; vertfact = Y__max/y_max;
}
```

We will add this function to our graphics module GRASPTC; we can call it only when the variables $X\_\_max$, $Y\_\_max$, and x_max have obtained their proper values, so we insert the following lines in the function *initgr*:

```
X__max = getmaxx(); Y__max = getmaxy();
x_max=10.0;
boundaries_uc();
```

The complete module GRASPTC is listed at the end of Chapter 3. We will use it with almost all our graphics programs, without mentioning this each time.

An interesting new aspect is that we can call the function *boundaries_uc* in our own programs to switch to other units of length. For example, if we want x_max to be 20.0, we can write

```
initgr();
x_max = 20.0;
boundaries_uc();
```

With a screen of about 20 cm wide, we can then call our user coordinates 'centimetres' (instead of inches). If we don't change the variable x_max, it will have the default value 10.0.

It is interesting to consider the values of all variables associated with the aspect ratio for various graphics adapters:

	HGA	CGA	EGA	VGA
X_max	719	639	639	639
Y_max	347	199	349	479
w	7 500	4 167	7 750	10 000
h	10 000	10 000	10 000	10 000
x_max	10.000	10.000	10.000	10.000
y_max	6.435	7.474	7.047	7.496
horfact	71.900	63.900	63.900	63.900
vertfact	53.925	26.627	49.522	63.900

These data were obtained by running program ASPRATIO, linked together with GRASPTC, on various machines with the graphics adapters mentioned in the headings in the above table. As you can see, the preliminary value $y\_max = 7.0$, used in Section 1.5 and in my previous graphics books, is very reasonable after all!

```
/* ASPRATIO: List various graphics constant values;
             The output of this program is machine dependent!
*/
#include "grasptc.h"

main()
{ int w, h;
  initgr();
  getaspectratio(&w, &h);
  endgr();
```

```
   printf("X__max=%d  Y__max=%d  w=%d  h=%d  x_max=%f  y_max=%f\n",
   X__max, Y__max, w, h, x_max, y_max);
   printf("horfact=%f  vertfact=%f", horfact, vertfact);
}
```

So far, we have assumed the values of w and h obtained by *getaspectratio* to be correct, so that our programs SQUARE1 and SQUARE2 really draw squares. If this is not the case on our machine because we are using non-standard hardware, we can make *getaspectratio* return values other than it normally does. We then have to call the Turbo C function *setaspectratio*, which in GRAPHICS.H is declared as follows:

```
   void far setaspectratio(int xasp, int yasp);
```

The parameters *xasp* and *yasp* correspond to our variables w and h, respectively. If we are also using our own function *initgr*, we should first call that function, then *setaspectratio*, and, finally, call *boundaries_uc*, so in that case we write, for example,

```
   initgr();
   setaspectratio(wnew, hnew);
   boundaries_uc();
```

First, when *initgr* is called, the global variables *horfact* and *vertfact* will obtain their normal values as a result of calling *getaspectratio*. Then *setaspectratio* supplies new values for w and h. Finally, in the function *boundaries_uc*, another call to *getaspectratio* follows, which now sets w and h to their new values, and with these the variables *horfact* and *vertfact* are computed once again, this time based on the new aspect ratio. These two variables are very important, since they are used in the functions *IX* and *IY*, which convert our user coordinates to the pixel coordinates required by Turbo C:

```
   int IX(float x)
   { return (int) (x * horfact + 0.5);
   }

   int IY(float y)
   { return Y__max - (int)(y * vertfact + 0.5);
   }
```

We will also define the functions *XPIX* and *YPIX*, which convert distances expressed in user coordinates to the corresponding number of pixels. For example, if a vertical side of a square is b 'inches' long, then it is *YPIX(b)* pixels long. Using *IY(b)* here would not be correct because of the opposite directions of the two y-axes. In the horizontal direction we have no such difficulty, so *XPIX(a) = IX(a)*:

```
int XPIX(float xdim)
{ return IX(xdim);
}

int YPIX(float ydim)
{ return (int)(ydim * vertfact + 0.5);
}
```

2.2 CIRCLES AND ARCS

In this section we will discuss some Turbo C functions that we can use to draw circles, arcs, and ellipses in a very efficient way. The prototypes of these functions are:

```
void far circle(int x, int y, int radius);
void far arc(int x, int y, int stangle, int endangle, int radius);
void far ellipse(int x, int y, int stangle, int endangle,
                 int xradius, int yradius);
void far getarccoords(struct arccoordstype far *arccoords);
```

The *arccoordstype* structure is defined in GRAPHICS.H as follows:

```
struct arccoordstype
{ int x, y;
  int xstart, ystart, xend, yend;
};
```

We can use function *circle* if both the pixel coordinates X and Y of its center and the radius are given. The radius, too, must be given as a number of pixels, on a horizontal radius! This is not exactly convenient, but as *circle* is a very fast function we will not abolish it but rather use it in the following function of our own, which is based on our user coordinates and therefore considerably easier to use:

```
void circle_uc(float x, float y, float r)
{ circle(IX(x), IY(y), XPIX(r));
}
```

With this function in module GRASPTC, we can use it, for example, as in program *MANYCIR*, which produces Fig. 2.1.

```
/* MANYCIR: This program draws many concentric circles.
*/
#include "grasptc.h"
```

```
main()
{ float xC, yC, d, rmax, r;
  printf("Distance, in inches (for example, 0.1):");
  scanf("%f", &d);
  initgr();
  xC = 0.5 * x_max; yC = 0.5 * y_max; rmax = 1.5;
  for (r=d; r<=rmax; r+=d)
    circle_uc(xC, yC, r);
  endgr();
}
```

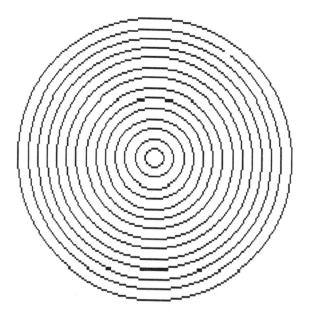

Fig. 2.1. Circles drawn by program MANYCIR

If you want to use function *setwritemode* with *XOR_PUT* as an argument, as discussed in Section 1.4, you will find that the Turbo C function *circle* will not pay attention to this but keep writing circles in the normal way. We will solve this problem in Section 2.7.

We can use the Turbo C function *arc* if we want to draw a circular arc. We then have to supply the start and the end angles, in degrees, where, as usual in mathematics, we measure the angles from the positive *x*-axis, and imagine the arc to be drawn counterclockwise. For example, if we write

```
arc(xC, yC, -90, 180, R);
```

we obtain three quarters of a circle, with center xC, yC and radius R, as shown in Fig. 2.2. Obviously, if we use a start angle of 0° and an end angle of 360°, we obtain a full circle. Note that all five arguments of *arc* are of type *int*. It is unfortunate that the start and the end angles are to be given as integers. A more general function to draw an arc will be discussed in Section 2.3.

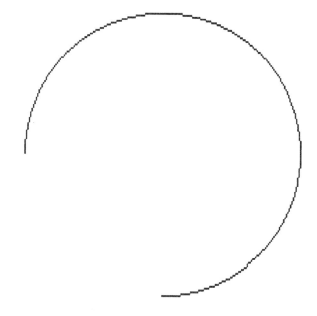

Fig. 2.2. Three quarters of circle

After a call of *arc*, the coordinates of the start and end positions of the arc drawn are immediately available. All we have to do to obtain them is to declare (or rather 'to define') a variable of the predefined type *struct arccoordstype* and to pass its address as an argument to the function *getarccoords*. In addition to the start and end positions of the arc, its center (x, y) will also be stored in the structure. Here is a simple demonstration program that draws a triangular box with rounded corners, as shown in Fig. 2.3.

```
/* BOX: A triangular box with round corners.
*/
#include "grasptc.h"

main()
{ float xleft, xright, ylower, yupper, r;
  int Xleft, Xright, Ylower, Yupper, R;
  struct arccoordstype P[3];
```

```
initgr();
xleft = x_max/2 - 1.0; xright = xleft + 2.0;
ylower = y_max/2 - 1.0; yupper = ylower + 2.0;
r = 0.5;
Xleft = IX(xleft); Xright = IX(xright);
Ylower = IY(ylower); Yupper = IY(yupper);
R = XPIX(r);

arc(Xleft, Ylower, 180, 270, R);
getarccoords(P);      /* Address of P[0] */

arc(Xright, Ylower, 270, 45, R);
getarccoords(P + 1); /* Address of P[1] */

arc(Xleft, Yupper, 45, 180, R);
getarccoords(P + 2); /* Address of P[2] */

line(P[0].xend, P[0].yend, P[1].xstart, P[1].ystart);
line(P[1].xend, P[1].yend, P[2].xstart, P[2].ystart);
line(P[2].xend, P[2].yend, P[0].xstart, P[0].ystart);
endgr();
}
```

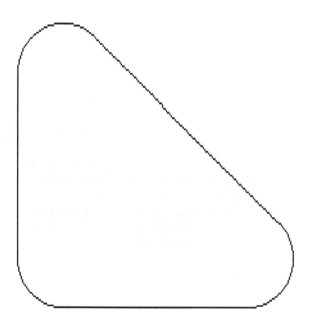

Fig. 2.3. Triangular box with rounded corners

As you saw at the beginning of this section, there is also a function for drawing an ellipse. As ellipses are less common than circles, there is only one function, *ellipse*, to draw both full ellipses and elliptic arcs. (Since a circular arc is a special case of an elliptic arc, any circle or arc that can be drawn by the functions *circle* and *arc* can also be drawn by the function *ellipse*!) As with *arc*, we have to supply both a start and an end angle. This function can only draw ellipses that have horizontal and vertical principal axes. Half the lengths of these principal axes are supplied as the fifth argument *xradius* and the sixth argument *yradius*. Program ELLARCS generates a square in which a large number of elliptic arcs are drawn, as Fig. 2.4 shows.

```
/* ELLARCS: Elliptic arcs.
*/

#include "grasptc.h"

main()
{ int n, i, j, RXmajor, RYmajor, RXminor, RYminor;
  float rmajor, rminor, xC, yC, x0, y0,
    xleft, xright, ylower, yupper, x, y, s, d;
  printf("How many elliptic arc pairs on each curve (e.g. 4)? ");
  scanf("%d", &n);
  printf("Major radius of one elliptic arc (e.g. 0.4):  ");
  scanf("%f", &rmajor);
  printf("Minor radius of one elliptic arc (e.g. 0.25): ");
  scanf("%f", &rminor);
  initgr();
  RXmajor = XPIX(rmajor);
  RYmajor = YPIX(rmajor);
  RXminor = XPIX(rminor);
  RYminor = YPIX(rminor);
  xC = 0.5 * x_max;
  yC = 0.5 * y_max;
  s = n * (rmajor + rminor);
  d = n * (rmajor - rminor);
  x0 = xC - s; y0 = yC - d;
  xleft = x0; xright = xC + s;
  ylower = yC - s; yupper = yC + s;
  rectangle(IX(xleft), IY(yupper), IX(xright), IY(ylower));
    /* All elliptic arcs lie inside the square just drawn. */
  for (i=0; i<=2*n; i++)
  for (j=0; j<2*n; j+=2)
  { x = x0 + i * rmajor + j * rminor;
    y = y0 + (j + 1) * rmajor - i * rminor;
    ellipse(IX(x), IY(y), 270, 360, RXminor, RYmajor);
    x += 2 * rminor;
```

```
    ellipse(IX(x), IY(y), 90, 180, RXminor, RYmajor);
  }
  for (j=0; j<=2*n; j++)
  for (i=0; i<2*n; i+=2)
  { x = x0 + (i + 1) * rmajor + j * rminor;
    y = y0 + j * rmajor - i * rminor;
    ellipse(IX(x), IY(y), 180, 270, RXmajor, RYminor);
    y -= 2 * rminor;
    ellipse(IX(x), IY(y), 0, 90, RXmajor, RYminor);
  }
  endgr();
}
```

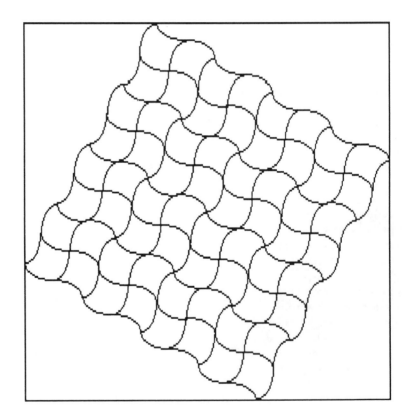

Fig. 2.4. Pattern of elliptic arcs

2.3 MORE ABOUT ARCS

As we have seen in the preceding section and elsewhere, the Turbo C graphics functions are rather low-level: they are fast but device dependent, and, especially because of aspect-ratio problems, not always pleasant to work with. The requirement that the start and end angles of arcs be expressed as integers, denoting numbers of degrees, might be very efficient but it is not very attractive from a mathematical point of view. In Section 2.2, we have used a very simple circle-drawing function (*circle_uc*) of our own, and we now want to develop a equally useful function *arc_uc*, to draw a circular arc with start and end angles given as float numbers and expressed in radians. Remember that the well-known C functions *cos* and *sin*, which we often need, also take arguments expressed in radians. In order to make *arc_uc* reasonably fast, we will base it on the Turbo C line-drawing functions. Thus, we will approximate an arc by a set of line segments, and supply an extra argument that says how many line segments are to be used. As with the Turbo C function *arc*, we will imagine the arc to be drawn counterclockwise, from the start angle to the end angle. Making the start and end positions of the arc available to the user may save some computing time, so we will borrow this idea from Turbo C and define both a structure type *arc_uctype*, similar to *arccoordstype*, and a function *getarc_uc*, similar to the Turbo C function *getarccoords*. We will insert the following program text in the header file GRASPTC.H:

```
#define PI 3.141592653589793

void arc_uc(float xC, float yC, float stangle,
            float endangle, float radius, int nlinesegments);

struct arc_uctype
{ float x, y, xstart, ystart, xend, yend;
};
```

Although this header file is primarily intended to be used in application programs, we can also use it in the file GRASPTC.C, to which we now add:

```
#include <math.h>
#include "grasptc.h"

static float xarc_C, yarc_C, xarc_start, yarc_start,
             xarc_end, yarc_end;

void arc_uc(float xC, float yC, float stangle,
            float endangle, float radius, int nlinesegments)
{ float theta, phi;
  int i;
```

```
    while (endangle < stangle) endangle += 2*PI;
    theta = (endangle - stangle)/nlinesegments;
    xarc_start = xC + radius*cos(stangle);
    yarc_start = yC + radius*sin(stangle);
    xarc_end = xC + radius*cos(endangle);
    yarc_end = yC + radius*sin(endangle);
    move(xarc_start, yarc_start);
    for (i=1; i<nlinesegments; i++)
    { phi = stangle + i * theta;
      draw(xC+radius*cos(phi), yC+radius*sin(phi));
    }
    draw(xarc_end, yarc_end);
    xarc_C = xC; yarc_C = yC;
}

void getarc_uc(struct arc_uctype *arccoords)
{ arccoords->x = xarc_C;
  arccoords->y = yarc_C;
  arccoords->xstart = xarc_start;
  arccoords->ystart = yarc_start;
  arccoords->xend = xarc_end;
  arccoords->yend = yarc_end;
}
```

With GRASPTC.H and GRASPTC.C thus updated, we can now write, for
example, program BOX1, listed below. It may seem to be as complicated as the
equivalent program BOX of Section 2.2, but it is easier to write because it uses
only one type of coordinate, and it can more easily be adapted to other situations
because angles are given as floating-point numbers rather than as integers.

```
/* BOX1: Triangular box with round corners, based on user coordinates.
*/
#include "grasptc.h"

main()
{ float xleft, xright, ylower, yupper, r;
  struct arc_uctype P[3];
  initgr();
  xleft = x_max/2 - 1.0; xright = xleft + 2.0;
  ylower = y_max/2 - 1.0; yupper = ylower + 2.0;
  r = 0.5;
  arc_uc(xleft, ylower, PI, 1.5*PI, r, 20);
  getarc_uc(P);      /* Address of P[0] */

  arc_uc(xright, ylower, 1.5*PI, PI/4, r, 25);
  getarc_uc(P + 1); /* Address of P[1] */
```

```
arc_uc(xleft, yupper, PI/4, PI, r, 25);
getarc_uc(P + 2); /* Address of P[2] */

line_uc(P[0].xend, P[0].yend, P[1].xstart, P[1].ystart);
line_uc(P[1].xend, P[1].yend, P[2].xstart, P[2].ystart);
line_uc(P[2].xend, P[2].yend, P[0].xstart, P[0].ystart);

endgr();
}
```

The output of program BOX1 is identical to that of program BOX, and is therefore already shown in Fig. 2.3. The new approach of program BOX1 has its price: it is much slower than program BOX.

An arc through three given points

Once we are relieved of the burden of thinking about pixels and the aspect ratio we can focus on subjects that are more interesting from the point of view of geometry. For example, let us write a function that, with three given points A, B, C, draws the (circular) arc that starts in A, passes through B, and ends in C. Obviously, A, B, and C must not lie on a straight line. We use the perpendicular bisectors of line segments AB and BC. The point of intersection of these two bisectors is the center O of the circle through A, B, and C. Figure 2.5 shows these points and these bisectors OD and OE. In many applications we have to construct a vector $\mathbf{n}$, perpendicular to a given vector $\mathbf{u}$. This is very easy if we are familiar with the notion of the dot product (or inner product) of two vectors. If we have

$$\mathbf{u} = [u_1 \quad u_2]$$

then we can use

$$\mathbf{n} = [n_1 \quad n_2] = [u_2 \quad -u_1]$$

as the desired perpendicular vector. We verify this by computing the dot product of the two vectors:

$$\mathbf{u} \cdot \mathbf{n} = u_1 n_1 + u_2 n_2 = u_1 u_2 + u_2(-u_1) = 0$$

Any two non-zero vectors with a zero dot product are perpendicular, so $\mathbf{n}$ can serve as the desired perpendicular vector. We apply this method twice to obtain the vectors $\mathbf{n}$ and $\mathbf{m}$, perpendicular to AB and BC, respectively. We also compute the midpoints D of AB and E of BC. With the coordinates of D and E given, we can now use the vectors $\mathbf{n}$ and $\mathbf{m}$ to compute O, the center of the circle through

A, B, and C. With $\mathbf{D} = [x_D \quad y_D]$, we can say that the line through point D, perpendicular to AB, has the vector representation

$$\mathbf{D} + \lambda\mathbf{n}$$

Analogously, the line through point E, perpendicular to BC, is written as

$$\mathbf{E} + \mu\mathbf{m}$$

These two perpendicular lines meet in O. We can find the values of λ and μ of this point of intersection by solving the vector equation

$$\mathbf{D} + \lambda\mathbf{n} = \mathbf{E} + \mu\mathbf{m}$$

which we can write as

$$x_D + \lambda n_1 = x_E + \mu m_1$$
$$y_D + \lambda n_2 = y_E + \mu m_2$$

We do not really need the value of μ, so we solve this set of equations for λ, and find

$$\lambda = \frac{m_2(x_E - x_D) - m_1(y_E - y_D)}{m_2 n_1 - m_1 n_2}$$

We can now compute the coordinates of point O:

$$x_O = x_D + \lambda n_1$$
$$y_O = y_D + \lambda n_2$$

With vector $\mathbf{OA} = \mathbf{r} = [x_A - x_O \quad y_A - y_O]$, we first compute the radius

$$r = \sqrt{(r_1^2 + r_2^2)}$$

and then the start angle of the arc. This angle is equal to $\arctan(r_2/r_1)$ if r_1 is positive, that is, if A lies to the right of O. If A lies to the left of O, as is the case in Fig. 2.5, we have to add π to that value. Finally, if A and O have the same x-coordinate, the angle is either $\pi/2$ or $3\pi/2$, depending on whether A lies above or below O. Our function *angle* computes this angle in a single conditional expression.

The denominator $m_2 n_1 - m_1 n_2$, used in the above computation of λ, can also be written as

$$Determinant = \begin{vmatrix} n_1 & m_1 \\ n_2 & m_2 \end{vmatrix}$$

We use this number not only to compute λ but also to determine whether the orientation of the three points A, B, C, in that order, is counterclockwise or clockwise. We would not need this if we had to draw a full circle, but now that we are drawing an arc, we must be careful: strictly speaking, we may not be able to draw the desired arc beginning at A and ending at C, for the elementary arc-drawing functions *arc* and *arc_uc* can only draw arcs counterclockwise. The points A, B, C, in that order, are counterclockwise if *Determinant* is positive, and clockwise if it is negative. In the latter case we can simply draw the arc in the opposite direction, that is, from C to A. Finally, if A, B, and C lie on a straight line, *Determinant* is zero. In that case we draw nothing at all. In each of the three possible cases our function *drawarc3* returns the value of *Determinant*, so that the user can see which case applies. Also, the radius may be of interest to the user, so we will return this through an additional parameter. Note that the user can obtain the position of the center O by calling *getarc_uc*, because the actual drawing of the arc is done by the *arc_uc* function.

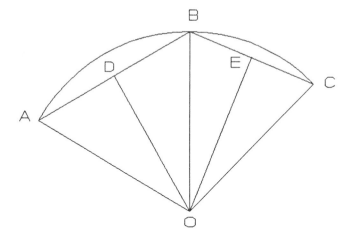

Fig. 2.5. Chords and perpendicular bisectors

We will add the following functions *angle* and *drawarc3* to GRASPTC:

```
float angle(float x, float y)
{ return (x > 0 ? atan(y/x) :
          x < 0 ? PI + atan(y/x) :
          y >= 0 ? PI/2 : 3*PI/2);
}
```

```c
float drawarc3(float xA, float yA,
               float xB, float yB,
               float xC, float yC,
               float *pr)
{ float u1, u2, n1, n2, xD, yD, v1, v2, m1, m2, xE, yE, lambda,
    xO, yO, r1, r2, r, stangle, endangle, phiA, phiC, determinant;
  int nsteps;
  u1 = xB - xA; u2 = yB - yA; /* Vector u points from A to B     */
  n1 = u2; n2 = -u1;              /* Vector n is perpendicular to u */
  xD = (xA+xB)/2; yD = (yA+yB)/2;         /* D is midpoint of AB */

  v1 = xC - xB; v2 = yC - yB; /* Vector v points from B to C     */
  m1 = v2; m2 = -v1;              /* Vector m is perpendicular to v */
  xE = (xB+xC)/2; yE = (yB+yC)/2;         /* E is midpoint of BC */
  determinant = m2*n1 - m1*n2;
  if (determinant == 0.0) return 0.0;
  lambda = (m2*(xE-xD) - m1*(yE-yD))/determinant;
                            /* Vector lambda.n points from D to O */
  xO = xD + lambda * n1;  /* O is center of circle through       */
  yO = yD + lambda * n2;  /* A, B, and C.                        */
  r1 = xA-xO; r2 = yA-yO; /* Vector (r1, r2) points from O to A */
  r = sqrt(r1*r1 + r2*r2);
  phiA = angle(r1, r2);
  phiC = angle(xC-xO, yC-yO);
  if (determinant > 0)
  { stangle = phiA; endangle = phiC;
  } else
  { stangle = phiC; endangle = phiA;
  }
  if (endangle < stangle) endangle += 2*PI;
  nsteps = (int)(r * (endangle - stangle) * 10) + 1;
    /* Number of steps dependent on both radius and angle */
  arc_uc(xO, yO, stangle, endangle, r, nsteps);
  *pr = r;
  return determinant;
}
```

Program ARC3 demonstrates the above function *drawarc3* (and the *angle* function used by it). The program marks the given points A, B, and C, as shown in Fig. 2.6. In this example the points A, B, C are clockwise, so actually the arc is drawn in the order C, B, A.

```
/* ARC3: Arc through three points A, B, C.
*/
#include <math.h>
#include "grasptc.h"

void mark(float x, float y, char *str)
{ float d=0.08;
  line_uc(x-d, y-d, x+d, y+d);
  line_uc(x-d, y+d, x+d, y-d);
  outtextxy(IX(x), IY(y)+10, str);
}

main()
{ float xA, yA, xB, yB, xC, yC, r;
  printf("Enter xA, yA, xB, yB, xC, yC:\n");
  scanf("%f %f %f %f %f %f", &xA, &yA, &xB, &yB, &xC, &yC);
  initgr();
  settextjustify(CENTER_TEXT, CENTER_TEXT);
  mark(xA, yA, "A"); mark(xB, yB, "B"); mark(xC, yC, "C");
  drawarc3(xA, yA, xB, yB, xC, yC, &r);
  endgr();
}
```

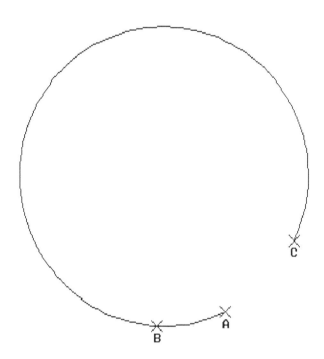

Fig. 2.6. Sample output of program ARC3

2.4 FILLETS

In mechanical engineering it is often required to replace sharp corners with *rounded* ones, as shown in Fig. 2.7. The arcs that replace the sharp corners are called *fillets*. In this very simple example, we have horizontal and vertical lines, which make the fillets very easy to draw.

Fig. 2.7. Box with fillets

We will not restrict ourselves to this simple case, but write a function that can draw a fillet for any corner. We will base the arc on a given radius r and three points A, B, and C, as shown in Fig. 2.8. The center O of the arc and its two end points D (on AB) and E (on BC) will be left in a global structure, in the same way as occurs in function *arc_uc* at the beginning of Section 2.3. Our function will not draw the straight line segments AD and EC. In this way, the user can give points A and C that, like point B, do not lie on the figure to be drawn. Two opposite corners of the original rectangle on which Fig. 2.7 is based are examples of such points A and C, and other examples will follow.

We now have to construct the positions of the points O, D, and E. We first compute the two vectors **n** and **m**, both of length 1, and pointing from B to A and C, respectively:

n = **BA**/BA
m = **BC**/BC

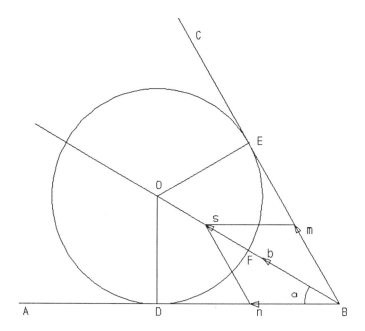

Fig. 2.8. Fillet construction

Notice the use of boldface for vectors in these formulae: **BA** is the vector with start point B and end point A, and BA is the length of that vector.

We compute the sum **s** of the vectors **n** and **m** and divide this new vector by its length $|s|$, so that the resulting vector **b** also has length 1:

$$\mathbf{s} = (\mathbf{n} + \mathbf{m})$$
$$\mathbf{b} = \mathbf{s}/|\mathbf{s}|$$

Vector **b** has the direction of the bisector of angle ABC. We use this to compute the position of point O, which lies on that bisector. Let us say that angle ABC is equal to 2α, so two angles α are formed by the bisector. Since radius r is equal to DO $=$ BO sin α, and vector **b** has length 1, we have the vector equality

$$\mathbf{BO} = \frac{r}{\sin \alpha} \mathbf{b}$$

We can find α by observing that vector **s**, already computed above, has length $2\cos \alpha$, so we use

$$\cos \alpha = \tfrac{1}{2}|s|$$
$$\sin \alpha = \sqrt{(1 - \cos^2 \alpha)}$$

The projection of vector **BO** on line BA is BD. Its length is equal to the dot product

BO · n

which we can use to find point D. We use that same length to compute the position of E analogously.

If we now had to use the function *arc_uc* we would have to compute the start and end angles, and to find out the orientation of the points A, B, C, in much the same way as we did when writing our function *drawarc3*. However, if we can find a third point on the arc we can use the latter function, and then we don't have to bother about those angles and that orientation. We use the point of intersection, F, of the arc and line BO for this purpose. Point F obviously lies at a distance r from O, and, since vector **b** is a unit vector, we have **OF** = $-r$**b**, which enables us to find the coordinates of F.

The following function *fillet* is based on the above analysis. Let us include it in module GRASPTC (and declare it in the header file GRASPTC.H).

```
float fillet(float xA, float yA, float xB, float yB,
      float xC, float yC, float r)
{ float n1, n2, m1, m2, BA, BC, s1, s2, length_of_s,
     b1, b2, cosa, sina, BO1, BO2, xO, yO, proj,
    xD, yD, xE, yE, xF, yF, q;
  n1 = xA - xB; n2 = yA - yB;
  BA = sqrt(n1*n1 + n2*n2);
  n1 /= BA; n2 /= BA;

  m1 = xC - xB; m2 = yC - yB;
  BC = sqrt(m1*m1 + m2*m2);
  m1 /= BC; m2 /= BC;

  s1 = n1 + m1; s2 = n2 + m2;
  length_of_s = sqrt(s1*s1 + s2*s2);
  b1 = s1/length_of_s; b2 = s2/length_of_s;
  cosa = length_of_s/2;
  sina = sqrt(1 - cosa*cosa); q = r/sina;
  BO1 = q * b1; BO2 = q * b2;
  xO = xB + BO1; yO = yB + BO2;
  proj = BO1 * n1 + BO2 * n2;
  xD = xB + proj * n1; yD = yB + proj * n2;
```

```
   xE = xB + proj * m1; yE = yB + proj * m2;
   xF = x0 - r * b1; yF = y0 - r * b2;
   return drawarc3(xD, yD, xF, yF, xE, yE, &r);
 }
```

We can then demonstrate this function by means of the following program, which has been used to produce Fig. 2.9.

```
/* FILLET: Function 'fillet' applied to an arbitrary triangle.
*/
#include <math.h>
#include "grasptc.h"

main()
{ float xA, yA, xB, yB, xC, yC, r, orientation;
  struct arc_uctype A, B, C;
  printf("Enter the coordinates xA, yA, xB, yB, xC, yC of\n");
  printf("the vertices A, B, C of a triangle.\n");
  printf("They must be counterclockwise.\n");
  scanf("%f %f %f %f %f %f", &xA, &yA, &xB, &yB, &xC, &yC);
  printf("Radius of fillet: "); scanf("%f", &r);
  initgr();
  orientation = fillet(xA, yA, xB, yB, xC, yC, r);
  if (orientation < 0)
  { closegraph();
    printf("A, B, C must be counterclockwise");
    exit(1);
  }
  getarc_uc(&B);
  fillet(xB, yB, xC, yC, xA, yA, r);
  getarc_uc(&C);
  fillet(xC, yC, xA, yA, xB, yB, r);
  getarc_uc(&A);
  line_uc(A.xend, A.yend, B.xstart, B.ystart);
  line_uc(B.xend, B.yend, C.xstart, C.ystart);
  line_uc(C.xend, C.yend, A.xstart, A.ystart);
  endgr();
}
```

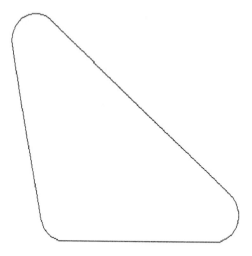

Fig. 2.9. Fillets in an arbitrary triangle

2.5 ENABLING PROGRAM BREAK

Sometimes we want to stop a running program, using Ctrl-Break or Ctrl-C. Unfortunately, if we take no special measures, pressing these keys may not have the desired effect. This is very annoying, especially when the computer is in the graphics mode, so we must do something about it. After all, now that the number of available graphics routines is rapidly increasing, the risk of our making errors resulting in endless loops also increases. Besides, we must also be able to terminate correct programs if they take much more time than we had expected. At the end of this section we will see an example where this may be the case.

There is a subtle distinction between Ctrl-Break and Ctrl-C, which I will mention shortly. At present, let us use the term *console break* for both key combinations. Turbo C offers the function *ctrlbrk*, which takes a function as its argument to prescribe which action is to be performed in the event of a console break. In our case, this function is not completely satisfactory, for two reasons:

1   The computer does not always obey our requests for a console break. It does when performing input and output by means of DOS routines, but it does not when accessing display memory, as in graphics output operations.

2   In unexpected situations many users may first press some other keys, such as the Enter key, and only if that has no effect will they press the Ctrl-C combination. If the characters entered in this way are not read by the program they are still in an input buffer when Ctrl-C is pressed, and will therefore cause that break request to be ineffective. (Ctrl-Break is different in that is clears the input buffer.)

The solution to the console-break problem we will discuss here is very efficient: apart from installing a special break handler during initialization and removing it on program termination, it does not require any action when the program is running. This is very important. Suppose, for example, that the program is calling the function *putpixel* to fill areas of the screen. Then it would not be efficient if with each of those calls (of which there may be many thousands) a special action had to be performed to investigate whether there is a console break.

Any time a key of the keyboard is pressed, a so-called *interrupt routine* (or *interrupt handler*) is executed. An interrupt routine is somewhat similar to a function. Its begin address is stored at some fixed location, called an *interrupt vector*, at the beginning of memory. There is a unique integer, 0, 1, 2, ... associated with each interrupt vector. As each vector is four bytes in length, the vector for interrupt 0 has address 0, that for interrupt 1 has address 4, and so on. The interrupt we are interested in has number 9, so its vector has address 4×9 = 36. In fact, we will not use that address ourselves. There are two Turbo C functions, *getvect* and *setvect*, declared in the header file DOS.H, to deal with interrupt vectors. Before we replace the old interrupt vector we save it in the pointer variable *oldInt9*, so that we can use and restore it later. We declare this pointer variable as follows:

```
static void interrupt (*oldInt9)(void);
```

Recall that the keyword *static* implies that the name *oldInt9* is known only in the current program module, which in our case will be GRASPTC. Without the new keyword *interrupt* this would be the declaration of a pointer to a function (instead of to an interrupt routine); the keyword *interrupt* also occurs in the definition of the new interrupt routine, *newInt9*, which has the form:

```
static void interrupt newInt9(void)
{ ...
}
```

(As its contents ... is rather complex, we will discuss this later.) We can then use the function *installBreak* shown below to install the new break handler, *newInt9*.

```
static int handler_installed=0;

void installBreak(void)
{ if (!handler_installed)
  { oldInt9 = getvect(9); setvect(9,newInt9);
    handler_installed = 1;
  }
}
```

We will call *installBreak* in our function *initgr*. The variable *handler_installed* indicates whether or not the new break handler is installed. After doing all our graphics work, we normally call our function *endgr*, and this is a good place to restore the old break handler by a call to the following function:

```
void restore_old_break(void)
{ if (handler_installed)
  { setvect(9, oldInt9); handler_installed = 0;
  }
}
```

Finally, we have to deal with the contents of the new interrupt handler, *newInt9*. Recall that this routine will immediately be called whenever a key is pressed. The first thing that must be done is to perform all the actions carried out by the old interrupt handler. We can use a pointer to a function in the same way as a function name, so we write

```
oldInt9();
```

As we have seen, any characters entered and not yet read by the program are available in a buffer. Normally this buffer is used as a queue, that is, 'first in, first out'. In our present case, however, the last character entered may be Ctrl-C, and if that is so we must use it and simply skip any previous characters. As we don't know if a console break has occurred, we must not simply start reading characters, using, say, *getch*, for then such characters disappear from the buffer and are no longer available to the program that may try to read them later.

We will therefore inspect the buffer itself. This is possible on the basis of the following information, which you can find, for example, in Peter Norton's *Programmer's Guide to the IBM PC*. The input buffer starts at address 0x41E. It is circular; let us use the terms *head* and *tail* to denote the oldest character to be used and the first free position, respectively. These are given as offsets from location 0x400, and can be found as integers at the addresses 0x41A and 0x41C. As we have

$$0x41E - 0x400 = 0x1E = 1 \times 16 + 14 = 30$$

the least value that will be found at the addresses 0x41A and 0x41C is 30. The buffer is 32 bytes long but can contain, at most, 16 characters, because each character is stored as two bytes, namely as an ASCII code, followed by a *scan code*. In our case, we are interested in Ctrl-C and Ctrl-Break, for which these codes are as follows:

	ASCII code	*Scan code*	*Integer value*
Ctrl-C	0x03	0x2E	0x2E03
Ctrl-Break	0x00	0x80	0x8000

Although the scan code is placed *after* the ASCII code, we obtain these two items in the reverse order if we combine the two bytes in one integer. (This is a well-known characteristic of the 8086 processor, which we normally need not bother about when programming in the C language.) This explains the third column of the above table, used in the following constant definitions:

```
#define CTRL_C 0x2E03
#define CTRL_BREAK 0x8000
```

Instead of comparing two bytes, we can now compare only one integer, which is faster. We will inspect the integer just preceding the buffer tail. As the buffer is circular, we must think of the special case when this tail corresponds to address 0x41E. If that happens, the logically preceding integer in the buffer is at the physical end of the buffer, that is, at location 0x41E + 30. Instead of using the original offset values 30, 32, ..., 60, we first reduce them by 30 and then divide them by 2 (in a shift-right operation). The latter is done because in an integer array, although the subscript is incremented by 1, the elements lie 2 bytes apart. This explains the calculation of the buffer location inspected in the function listed below:

```
static int *keybuffer  = (int *)0x41E;
static int *buffertail = (int *)0x41C;

static void interrupt newInt9(void)
{ unsigned int tail, code;
  oldInt9();
  /* *buffertail = 30, 32, ..., 60 */
  tail = (*buffertail - 30) >> 1;
  /* tail = 0, 1, ..., 15 */
  code = keybuffer[tail ? tail - 1 : 15];
  if (code == CTRL_C || code == CTRL_BREAK)
  { to_text(); exit(1);
  }
}
```

It should be noted that our interrupt handler is not made memory resident, so it is no longer in memory when the graphics program that installed it has finished and a new program has been started. It would then not be correct if the interrupt vector (in low memory, at address 36) still contained a pointer to our *newInt9* routine. Calling the function *restore_old_break* is therefore very essential. We will add the following function, *to_text*, to GRASPTC, and use it in *endgr*, an updated version of which is also listed below:

```
void to_text(void)
{ closegraph();
  restore_old_break();
}

void endgr(void)
{ getch();
  to_text();
}
```

As you have seen, a call of *to_text* also occurs in the above interrupt routine, *newInt9*. Thus, if we want to return to text mode immediately we use *to_text*, and if we want the user to press some key before switching back to text mode we use *endgr*. In either case the original break handler is restored.

So much for the rather technical subject of installing and restoring interrupt handlers.

As mentioned at the beginning of this section, a console break may be desirable not only for programs with endless loops but also for those that take a very long time. Especially with very general programs, this may be the case if our input data do not lead to satisfactory results. If the entire computer screen is to be filled by a pattern, we usually need to see only a small portion of it to decide if it is worth continuing. Program SPIRALS on the next page is a good example. With the input data suggested by the program itself, the pattern of Fig. 2.10 will be the result, but if you enter other input data, the program may take a lot of time. If then the pattern on the screen is not what you want, you can press Ctrl-Break or Ctrl-C to stop the program.

```
/* SPIRALS: Pattern of spirals
*/
#include <math.h>
#include "grasptc.h"

int narc, nline;
float rmax, n, halfpi, c, r0, delta;

float radius(float phi)
{ return c * phi + r0;
}

spirals4(float x, float y)
{ int i, j, l;
  float phi0, phi, r, phi_offset;
  for (l=0; l<4; l++)
  { phi0 = l*halfpi;
    move(x+r0*cos(phi0), y+r0*sin(phi0));
    for (i=0; i<narc; i++)
    for (j=1; j<=nline; j++)
    { phi_offset = i * halfpi + j * delta;
      phi = phi0 + phi_offset;
      r = radius(phi_offset);
      draw(x+r*cos(phi), y+r*sin(phi));
    }
  }
}

main()
{ float x, y, rmax;
  halfpi = PI/2;
  printf("How many line segments on a spiral arc of "
         "90 degrees? (e.g. 12): ");
  scanf("%d", &nline);
  printf("How many spiral arc segments of 90 degrees on each spiral?"
         " (e.g. 3) :");
  scanf("%d", &narc);
  printf("Radius r is computed as follows: r = c * phi + r0\n");
  printf("(phi in radians, r and r0 in inches).\n");
  printf("Enter c and r0 (e.g. 0.15  0): ");
  scanf("%f %f", &c, &r0);
  delta = halfpi/nline; rmax = radius(narc * halfpi);
  initgr();
  for (x=0.2+rmax; x<=x_max-rmax-0.1999; x+=2*rmax)
  for (y=0.2+rmax; y<=y_max-rmax-0.1999; y+=2*rmax) spirals4(x, y);
  endgr();
}
```

Fig. 2.10. Pattern of spirals

2.6 AREA FILLING

There are two Turbo C functions for drawing polygons: *drawpoly* draws a polygon in the usual way, and *fillpoly* both draws the polygon and fills its interior. Their declarations (in GRAPHICS.H) are

```
void far drawpoly(int numpoints, int far *polypoints);
void far fillpoly(int numpoints, int far *polypoints);
```

You may wonder if it is really worth paying attention to *drawpoly*; after all, our normal line-drawing functions already enable us to draw polygons. However, *fillpoly* is very interesting, and as *drawpoly* has the same arguments, it takes very little extra effort to discuss the latter function as well. The first argument, *numpoints*, denotes the number of coordinate pairs (X_i, Y_i) that are given through the second argument, *polypoints*. If the polygon has n vertices (numbered 0, 1, ..., $n - 1$), then *numpoints* should be equal to $n + 1$ and *polypoints* is the begin address of the following sequence of integers:

$$X_0, Y_0, X_1, Y_1, ..., X_{n-1}, Y_{n-1}, X_0, Y_0$$

Thus, we have to close the polygon ourselves by writing one coordinate pair twice, as is done here with point (X_0, Y_0); as a result, both the first argument, *numpoints*, and the number of coordinate pairs are equal to $n + 1$. (The Turbo

C Reference Manual contradicts itself on the correct value of *numpoints*, and the example it gives is very confusing on this point.) Note that we are using (integer) pixel coordinates again.

Both functions start drawing the polygon given through their arguments; after having drawn it, the task of *drawpoly* is completed, whereas *fillpoly* will fill it with a given fill pattern and with a given color. To specify what we want we must be familiar with a new function, declared in GRAPHICS.H as follows:

```
void setfillstyle(int pattern, int color);
```

We use this function to specify which pattern and color are to be used in the area-filling process. There are twelve standard patterns, numbered 0, 1, ..., 11, for which we can use symbolic constants:

Name	Value
EMPTY_FILL	0
SOLID_FILL	1
LINE_FILL	2
LTSLASH_FILL	3
SLASH_FILL	4
BKSLASH_FILL	5
LTBKSLASH_FILL	6
HATCH_FILL	7
XHATCH_FILL	8
INTERLEAVE_FILL	9
WIDE_DOT_FILL	10
CLOSE_DOT_FILL	11

(In most cases these twelve predefined fill patterns will suffice. If not, you can define your own fill pattern, using the Turbo C function *setfillpattern*. Consult the Turbo C Reference Guide if you need this function.)

The patterns 0, 1, ..., 11 are produced by program FILLDEMO and are shown in Fig. 2.11.

Fig. 2.11. Fill patterns

```
/* FILLDEMO: Demonstration of using standard fill patterns.
*/

#include <stdio.h>
#include "grasptc.h"

main()
{ int i, rctangle[10], foregroundcolor, width, XA, YA, XB, YB,
    XC, YC, XD, YD, displacement, txtheight, Xmax, Ymax;
  char str[3];
  printf("Enter Xmax and Ymax (for example, 600 200): ");
  scanf("%d %d", &Xmax, &Ymax);
  initgr();
  settextjustify(CENTER_TEXT, TOP_TEXT);
  settextstyle(TRIPLEX_FONT, HORIZ_DIR, 2);
  txtheight = textheight("A");
  width = Xmax/12;
  XA = XD = 0;
  XB = XC = width;
  YC = YD = txtheight + 8;
  YA = YB = Ymax;
  rctangle[1] = YA;
  rctangle[3] = YB;
  rctangle[5] = YC;
  rctangle[7] = YD;
  rctangle[9] = YA;
  foregroundcolor = getcolor();
  for (i=0; i<12; i++)
  { displacement = 1 + i * width;
    sprintf(str, "%2d", i);
```

```
      outtextxy(width/2 + displacement, 0, str);
      rctangle[0] = XA + displacement;
      rctangle[2] = XB+ displacement;
      rctangle[4] = XC + displacement;
      rctangle[6] = XD + displacement;
      rctangle[8] = rctangle[0];
      setfillstyle(i, foregroundcolor);
      fillpoly(5, rctangle);
   }
   endgr();
}
```

If you want to see area filling in action with polygons that are more complex than rectangles you can use program POLFILL. This can draw a quite complex polygon (which is the area between two spirals), and then fill it with a given standard fill pattern:

```
/* POLFILL: Filling a very complicated polygon.
*/

#include <stdio.h>
#include <math.h>
#include <alloc.h>
#include <stdlib.h>
#include "grasptc.h"

main()
{ int n, N, pattern, *points, i, k;
  float angle, theta, dr, cosith, sinith, x1, y1, x2, y2,
        r1, r2, xC, yC, xmax, ymax;
  printf("The polygon (in the form of a spiral) will have"
         " 2n vertices. Enter n: ");
  scanf("%d", &n);
  printf("Enter xmax and ymax (for example, 10.0 7.0): ");
  scanf("%f %f", &xmax, &ymax);
  N = 2 * n;
  printf("Fill-pattern number (less than 12): ");
  scanf("%d", &pattern);
  printf("Elementary angle in degrees (for example, 20): ");
  scanf("%f", &angle);
  theta = angle * PI/180;
  k = PI/theta;
  points = (int *)malloc(2 * (N+1) * sizeof(int));
  if (points == NULL) {printf("Memory problem"); exit(1);}
  initgr();
  xC = 0.5 * xmax; yC = 0.5 * ymax;
  setfillstyle(pattern, getcolor());
```

```
  dr = 0.3 * xmax / n;
  for (i=0; i<n; i++)
  { r1 = i * dr;
    r2 = (i + k) * dr;
    cosith = cos(i * theta);
    sinith = sin(i * theta);
    x1 = xC + r1 * cosith; y1 = yC + r1 * sinith;
    x2 = xC + r2 * cosith; y2 = yC + r2 * sinith;
    points[2*i] = IX(x1);
    points[2*i+1] = IY(y1);
    points[2*(N-1)-2*i] = IX(x2);
    points[2*(N-1)-2*i+1] = IY(y2);
  }
  points[2*N] = points[0];
  points[2*N+1] = points[1];
  fillpoly(N+1, points);
  endgr();
}
```

Figure 2.12 shows the output of this program, executed with n = 200 (so the polygon has 400 vertices!), *pattern* = 1 = *SOLID_FILL*, and *angle* = 20 (degrees).

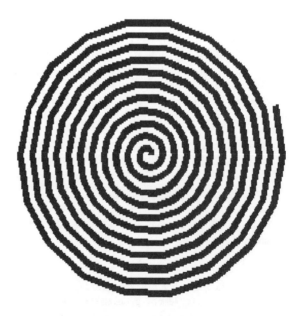

Fig. 2.12. Filled polygon

We can use the available fill patterns for various kinds of shading, as illustrated in Fig. 2.13. This figure shows a 'magic triangle', as drawn by M. C. Escher. Here it has been produced by program MAGTRIA, listed below.

```
/* MAGTRIA: Magic triangle.
*/
#include <math.h>
#include "grasptc.h"

main()
{ float a, b, ha, hb, c, s, sq3, xC, yC, x[6], y[6], xj, yj, r, w;
  int points[14], i, j, foregrcolor, fillpattern;
  printf("Side of innermost triangle (for example, 2.5): ");
  scanf("%f", &a); ha = 0.5 * a;
  sq3 = sqrt(3.0); r = ha * sq3/3.0;
  /* r is radius of circle inscribed in inner triangle.
  */
  c = -0.5;      /* cos 120 degr. */
  s = 0.5 * sq3; /* sin 120 degr. */
  printf("Enter thickness of each filled triangle (for example, 0.5): ");
  scanf("%f", &w);
  b = w/s;
  /* b is length of sides of the three small
     triangles that are cut off at the vertices
     of the largest triangle.
  */
  hb = 0.5 * b;
  initgr();
  xC = 0.5 * x_max; yC = 0.5 * (y_max - r);
  x[0] = -ha - 2 * b - hb; y[0] = -r - w;
  x[1] = x[0] + hb; y[1] = -r - 2 * w;
  x[2] = -x[1]; y[2] = y[1];
  x[3] = hb; y[3] = 2 * r + w;
  x[4] = 0.0; y[4] = 2 * r;
  x[5] = ha + hb; y[5] = y[0];
  foregrcolor = getcolor();
  for (i=0; i<3; i++)
  { for (j=0; j<6; j++)
    { xj = x[j]; yj = y[j];
      points[2*j] = IX(xC + xj);
      points[2*j+1] = IY(yC + yj);
      x[j] = c * xj - s * yj;
      y[j] = s * xj + c * yj;
      /* A rotation through 120 degr. for the next value of i.
      */
    }
    points[12] = points[0]; points[13] = points[1];
    fillpattern =
```

```
      (i == 0 ? SOLID_FILL :
       i == 1 ? INTERLEAVE_FILL :
                WIDE_DOT_FILL);
      setfillstyle(fillpattern, foregrcolor);
      fillpoly(7, points);
   }
   endgr();
}
```

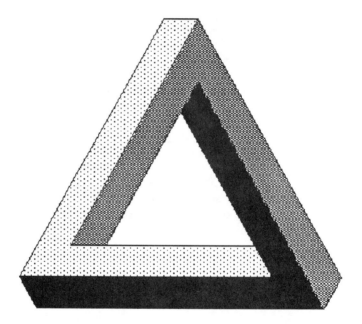

Fig. 2.13. Magic triangle

Filled circles and ellipses

In Turbo C Version 2.0 (not in Version 1.5) we can draw a filled circle or ellipse using the function *fillellipse*, declared in GRAPHICS.H as

```
void far fillellipse(int x, int y, int xradius, int yradius);
```

Like *fillpoly*, it uses the current fill color and fill pattern. Note that *fillellipse* is similar to *ellipse* as regards its parameters. Despite its name, *fillellipse* will probably be used more often for circles, such as those in Fig. 2.14, than for (non-circular) ellipses. (However, the name *fillellipse* is correct because a circle is a special case of an ellipse.)

The following function is based on our user coordinates. We will add it to GRASPTC, and insert its declaration in GRASPTC.H:

```
void fillcircle_uc(float x, float y, float radius)
{ fillellipse(IX(x), IY(y), XPIX(radius), YPIX(radius));
}
```

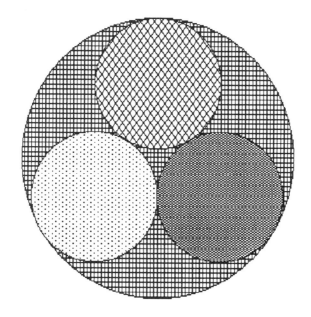

Fig. 2.14. Four filled circles

In addition to filling polygons and ellipses, we can fill any bounded region using the Turbo C function *floodfill*, declared in GRAPHICS.H as follows:

```
void far floodfill(int x, int y, int border);
```

Like *polyfill*, function *floodfill* uses the current fill pattern and fill color (normally specified by a previous call of *setfillstyle*). The arguments x and y are the coordinates of the 'seed point', that is, a point where filling can start. With only Turbo C 1.5, we could fill a circle either by using *floodfill* or by approximating circles by regular polygons (see Section 2.7) and using *fillpoly*. Now that the function *fillellipse* is available in Version 2.0, we should no longer use *floodfill* for circles. The Turbo C manual says:

Use *fillpoly* instead of *floodfill* whenever possible so that you can maintain code compatibility with future versions.

It also says that *floodfill* does not work with the IBM-8514 driver.

With 'flood fill' methods we always have to be very careful. The filling process continues in all directions until pixels with the color *border* are reached. Thus it is essential that point (x, y) lies in an area bounded by a curve of the color *border* (see Section 1.3 for the integer values of *border*). Sometimes a region looks 'closed' but is not really so because somewhere one pixel is missing. In that case 'bleeding' will occur, which means that the filling process does not terminate properly and destroys everything on our screen. We will therefore not discuss an example of *floodfill* but will restrict ourselves to *fillpoly* and *fillellipse*.

2.7 CIRCLES AND REGULAR POLYGONS

Circles approximated by polygons

As *circle* and *circle_uc*, discussed in Section 2.2, are good functions to draw circles, it may not seem a good idea to discuss circle approximations that are in fact only regular polygons. Yet there are reasons for doing this. First, the XOR write mode, discussed in Section 1.4, does not apply to the circle functions just mentioned. Since they do apply to the line-drawing functions, we can invert all pixels of any circle that is approximated by line segments. Another reason will be clear in Chapter 3, where we will save graphics results in files.

The most straightforward way of drawing a regular polygon of, say, 80 vertices (which is sometimes called an *80-gon*) is using the functions *cos* and *sin* for each of these vertices, as in:

```
void circle80slow(float xC, float yC, float r)
/* Circle, approximated by a 80-gon (preliminary version)
*/
{ int i;
  float delta=2*PI/80, theta=0;
  move(xC+r, yC);
  for (i=1; i<=80; i++)
  { theta += delta;
    draw(xC + r * cos(theta), yC + r * sin(theta));
  }
}
```

Of course, the value 80, chosen for the number of vertices, is quite arbitrary. The 'circle' will be drawn faster if you reduce this value, but then the approximation will be worse, especially for large circles. Another improvement with regard to speed, with no concession to the quality of the approximation, is based on the well-known trigonometric relations

$$\cos(\theta + \delta) = \cos \theta \cos \delta - \sin \theta \sin \delta$$
$$\sin(\theta + \delta) = \sin \theta \cos \delta + \cos \theta \sin \delta$$

These enable us to compute all required values of $\cos \theta$ and $\sin \theta$ without using the corresponding values of θ, let alone calling the rather time-consuming functions *cos* and *sin*. The only values that must be known at the start are $\cos \delta$ and $\sin \delta$, which we can write as constants in our function (again using $\delta = 2\pi/80$). Function *circle80faster* will be considerably faster than *circle80slow*, and also offers the possibility of filling the polygon with the current fill pattern and color; it will do so if its fourth argument, *fill*, is non-zero.

```
#define COSDELTA 0.996917333733
#define SINDELTA 0.078459095728

void circle80faster(float xC, float yC, float r, int fill)
/* Circle, approximated by a 80-gon
   (improved, but still preliminary version)
*/
{ double costh=1.0, sinth=0.0, c0, s0;
  int j=0, XC, YC, H, V, points[162];
  XC = IX(xC); YC = IY(yC);
  for (j=0; j<=40; j+=2)
  { H = XPIX(r * costh);
    V = YPIX(r * sinth);
    points[j] = XC+H; points[j+1] = YC+V;
    if (j) {points[160-j] = XC+H; points[161-j] = YC-V;}
    if (j != 40)
    { points[80-j] = XC-H; points[81-j] = YC+V;
      if (j) {points[80+j] = XC-H; points[81+j] = YC-V;}
    }
    c0 = costh; s0 = sinth;
    costh = c0 * COSDELTA - s0 * SINDELTA;
    sinth = s0 * COSDELTA + c0 * SINDELTA;
  }
  points[160] = points[0]; points[161] = points[1];
  if (fill) fillpoly(81, points); else drawpoly(81, points);
}
```

Although *circle80faster* is already much faster than *circle80slow*, we can still improve it considerably. In its present form we use floating-point arithmetic to compute the elements of array *points* for each circle to be drawn. However, we can consider each circle to be derived from some 'standard circle', with a fixed radius and, say, with the origin (0, 0) as its center. It is therefore possible to use another array, which we will call *stdpoints*, with data for this standard circle. We will do this only for the first circle that is drawn. The C language offers us an excellent opportunity to do this, namely the concept of *static* variables. We will write two versions, a fast one, *circle80_pc*, based on pixel coordinates, and a convenient one, *circle80_uc*, based on user coordinates:

```
#include "grasptc.h"
#define COSDELTA 0.996917333733
#define SINDELTA 0.078459095728

void circle80_pc(int XC, int YC, int R)
/* Circle, approximated by regular 80-gon, based on pixel coordinates
*/
{ static int first=1, stdpoints[162];
  int j=0, H, V, points[162];
  double costh, sinth, c0, s0;
  checkbreak();
  if (first)
  { first = 0; costh = 1.0; sinth = 0.0;
    for (j=0; j<=40; j+=2)
    { H = (int)(1e4 * costh + 0.5);
      V = (int)(1e4 * sinth * vertfact/horfact + 0.5);
      stdpoints[j] = H; stdpoints[j+1] = V;
      if (j) {stdpoints[160-j] = H; stdpoints[161-j] = -V;}
      if (j != 40)
      { stdpoints[80-j] = -H; stdpoints[81-j] = V;
        if (j) {stdpoints[80+j] = -H; stdpoints[81+j] = -V;}
      }
      c0 = costh; s0 = sinth;
      costh = c0 * COSDELTA - s0 * SINDELTA;
      sinth = s0 * COSDELTA + c0 * SINDELTA;
    }
    stdpoints[160] = stdpoints[0];
    stdpoints[161] = stdpoints[1];
  }

  for (j=0; j<=160; j+=2)
  { points[j] = XC + (int)(stdpoints[j]*(long)R/10000L);
    points[j+1] = YC + (int)(stdpoints[j+1]*(long)R/10000L);
    if (j) invertpixel(points[j], points[j+1]);
    /* Necessary in case of XOR_PUT */
  }
  drawpoly(81, points);
}
```

```
void circle80_uc(float xC, float yC, float r)
/* Circle, approximated by regular 80-gon, based on user coordinates
*/
{ circle80_pc(IX(xC), IY(yC), XPIX(r));
}
```

As discussed at the beginning of this section, we want the above functions to be 'write-mode sensitive', that is, after the call

```
setwritemode(XOR_PUT)
```

our two new circle-drawing functions should invert the pixels on the circle that is being drawn, so that drawing the same circle twice causes a circle to appear and to disappear. Unfortunately, if two adjacent sides AB and BC of a polygon are drawn with the XOR_PUT write mode, then vertex B is used twice, which makes it appear and disappear (or vice versa). Thus we would obtain a polygon without the pixels at its vertices. The remedy used in *circle80_pc* is to visit these vertices once more: we call *invertpixel* for the vertices before we call *drawpoly*. In the normal COPY_PUT write mode this is superfluous (but harmless), since the vertices are also covered when *drawpoly* is called later. In the XOR_PUT write mode, however, the vertices will now altogether be visited three times, which has the same effect as visiting them once.

The *circle80_pc* function is used in BBALL, a simple *animation* program. This simulates a bouncing ball, which moves along straight lines in a rectangle at angles of 45° to the sides of the rectangle, reflecting each time like a real bouncing ball. The program is extended in that it can display any number of successive ball positions. So the path the ball follows is a broken line which first grows at one end until it has its prescribed length, and then both grows at one end and shrinks at the other. As pixels are inverted, there is an odd effect at the intersections of any two paths, where two circles coincide: the second circle will erase the first, as Fig. 2.15 shows. However, when one of the two intersecting paths disappears, the other circle is restored, so the damage is only temporary. Illustrations in books are static, so they do not really show how objects move on the screen. Yet in Fig. 2.15 you can see that the screen was 'captured' when something was happening: in the left half of the picture you see a very small portion of a circle that was being drawn at that moment. In the next chapter we will discuss 'screen captures' in more detail.

```c
/* BBALL: A bouncing ball
*/
#include <conio.h>
#include <stdio.h>
#include "grasptc.h"

main()
{ int R, h, left, right, top, bottom, X, Y, dX, dY, X0, Y0,
  dX0, dY0, n, k=0, Xmax, Ymax, starting=1;
  printf("Enter Xmax and Ymax (for example, 600 190): ");
  scanf("%d %d", &Xmax, &Ymax);
  printf("Enter the radius (for example, 10): ");
  scanf("%d", &R);
  printf("How many circles do you want to be visible at the same time? ");
  scanf("%d", &n);
  printf("\nAfter you have seen enough bouncing balls,\n");
  printf("press Ctrl-C to quit.\n\n");
  printf("Press any key ...");  getch();
  initgr();
  h = (int)(R * vertfact/horfact + 0.5);
  dX0 = dX = (int)(2 * R + 0.5);
  dY0 = dY = (int)(2 * h + 0.5);
  Xmax = ((Xmax - 2*R)/dX) * dX + 2*R;
  Ymax = ((Ymax - 2*h)/dY) * dY + 2*h;
   /* To ensure that the ball will touch the edges */
  rectangle(0, 0, Xmax, Ymax);
  left = R;  right = Xmax - R;
  top = h;  bottom = Ymax - h;
  X0 = X = 5 * R;  Y0 = Y = h;  /* Just some start point */
  k=0;
  setwritemode(XOR_PUT);
  while (!kbhit())
  { if (X + dX < left || X + dX > right) dX = -dX;
    if (Y + dY < top || Y + dY > bottom) dY = -dY;
    X += dX;  Y += dY;
    circle80_pc(X, Y, R);  /* Draw new circle  */
    if (starting && ++k == n) starting = 0;
    if (! starting)
    { /* There are now n circles visible */
      if (X0 + dX0 < left || X0 + dX0 > right) dX0 = -dX0;
      if (Y0 + dY0 < top || Y0 + dY0 > bottom) dY0 = -dY0;
      X0 += dX0;  Y0 += dY0;
      circle80_pc(X0, Y0, R); /* Erase old circle */
      k = n;
    }
  }
  to_text();
}
```

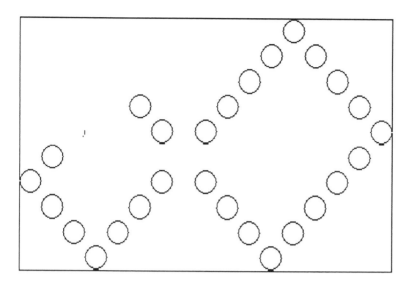

Fig. 2.15. Positions of a bouncing ball

2.8 LINES OF ANY WIDTH

In Turbo C we can draw several types of lines by using the function *setlinestyle*, declared in *graphics.h* as follows:

```
void far setlinestyle(int linestyle, unsigned upattern, int thickness);
```

The first argument, *linestyle*, can be one of the following five values, for which we may write the given symbolic constants:

Value	Symbolic constant
0	SOLID_LINE
1	DOTTED_LINE
2	CENTER_LINE
3	DASHED_LINE
4	USERBIT_LINE

The second argument, *upattern*, is used only if the first argument is equal to *USERBIT_LINE*. Otherwise, it is ignored. (Note that even in that case a value, for example, 0, must be supplied.) If the first argument is equal to the value *USERBIT_LINE*, then the 16 bits of *upattern* are used as a pattern. For every one-bit in *upattern* a pixel will be given the foreground color, and the pattern is repeated if the line is longer than 16 pixels.

The third argument, *thickness*, says how thick the lines will be. Unfortunately. there are only two possibilities for this argument:

Value	Symbolic constant	
1	*NORM_WIDTH*	(1 pixels wide)
3	*THICK_WIDTH*	(3 pixels wide)

A call of *setlinestyle* applies to all subsequent calls of Turbo C functions that draw lines, circles, arcs, etc.

Very thick lines, rounded end points

Turbo C has no built-in facilities to draw lines wider than three pixels. It is an interesting and useful exercise to write a function that can draw a (solid) line of any thickness. In doing this, we have to pay special attention to the end points of each line. This is important, especially if the end point of one line is the start point of another, which is very often the case. In such cases it would be wrong to draw line AB with thickness d simply as a rectangle with length AB and width d, as Fig. 2.16 shows. You can see the result of ignoring the end-point problem in Fig. 2.17, in the object on the left.

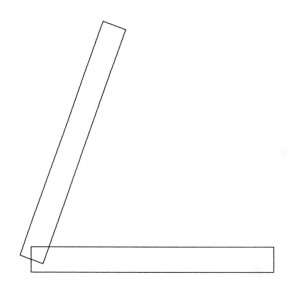

Fig. 2.16. Incorrect joint

An elegant solution to this problem is based on the idea of drawing filled circles each of which has an end point (A or B) as its center and $d/2$ as its radius. (This idea was suggested to me in a letter that I received from Nikita Andreiev from ConsulTek, Inc., San Carlos, CA, USA.) With our function *fillcircle_uc*, this task is extremely simple. At the end of this section you find program FATDEMO; this program calls the function *fatline*, in which this principle was used. The object in the middle of Fig. 2.17 shows the rounded corners obtained in this way.

Fig. 2.17. Fat lines in three styles

There is also a function *fatline0*, which merely draws a filled rectangle, with identical parts on either side of the given line P_1, P_2. The length of this rectangle is equal to the length of line segment $P_1 P_2$. Function *fatline*, after calling *fatline0*, draws two filled circles with P_1 and P_2 as their centers. Note that the way function *fatline* draws a thick line is independent of any other lines that may join this line at its end points. This will be different in the next section.

Very thick lines, sharp joints

Figure 2.17 was produced by program FATDEMO, listed at the end of this section. It shows three quadrangles, drawn with thick lines. The incorrect one on the left is the result of using only *fatline0*. The one in the middle was drawn with *fatline*, which gives rounded joints. The one on the right, with sharp joints, is the subject of this section. In order to obtain a set of functions that are easy to use we store the end points given as arguments in calls to *fatline0*, so that we can use them in a subsequent call of a new function, *sharpjoint*. (This saves us the trouble of supplying the x- and y-coordinates of three end points once again.)

As shown in Fig. 2.18, *sharpjoints* has the task of drawing and filling the quadrangle DEBF. Besides $d = 2r$, given as an argument, it can use the x- and y-coordinates of the points A, B, and C, stored previously in global variables. (Note that we will eventually implement this idea by using global static variables in our graphics module; then they cannot be accessed directly in any user's program, so there is no danger of these being modified by accident.)

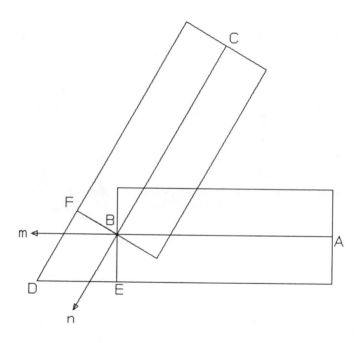

Fig. 2.18. Quadrangle DEBF

If we divide the vectors **BA** and **BC** by their lengths and supply them with a minus sign, we then obtain two very useful unit vectors:

$$\mathbf{m} = [m_1 \ m_2] = -\mathbf{BA}/\mathbf{BA}$$
$$\mathbf{n} = [n_1 \ n_2] = -\mathbf{BC}/\mathbf{BC}$$

The angle β at point B and between the lines BA and BC is also the angle between the vectors **m** and **n**, and could therefore be derived from the inner product

$$\mathbf{m} \cdot \mathbf{n} = \cos \beta$$

For our purposes, we need neither $\cos \beta$ nor β itself but rather $\sin \beta$, which we can compute directly as a vector product:

$$|\mathbf{m} \times \mathbf{n}| = \sin \beta$$

(We will briefly discuss this vector product below, when discussing whether or not A, B, C, in that order, are counterclockwise.) After having found $\sin \beta$, we compute

$$\mathbf{BD} = (r/\sin \beta)(\mathbf{m} + \mathbf{n})$$

where r is half the given line width w. Adding this vector to the coordinates of point B gives us the position of point D (see Fig. 2.18).

Similarly, we find points E and F by means of the vectors $\mathbf{BE}$ and $\mathbf{BF}$. Vector $\mathbf{BE}$ has length r, and is perpendicular to the unit vector $\mathbf{m} = [m_1 \; m_2]$. We now have to face the problem that both $[m_2 \; -m_1]$ and $[-m_2 \; m_1]$ are unit vectors perpendicular to $\mathbf{m}$ (which you can check by means of their inner products with $\mathbf{m}$), so which is the one to choose in our case? Here we have to take the orientation of the three points A, B, and C into account. If these three points are counterclockwise (see below), we have

$$\mathbf{BE} = r\,[-m_2 \quad m_1], \qquad \mathbf{BF} = r\,[n_2 \quad -n_1]$$

otherwise, we have

$$\mathbf{BE} = r\,[m_2 \quad -m_1], \qquad \mathbf{BF} = r\,[-n_2 \quad n_1]$$

(You can use 2×2 matrices for rotations about B through angles $90°$ and $-90°$ to find this.)

Thus, the only remaining problem is to determine the orientation of the points A, B, and C. For this, again we use the vectors $\mathbf{m}$ and $\mathbf{n}$. The point sequence {B, A, C} is counterclockwise (as in Fig. 2.18) if and only if a rotation of vector $\mathbf{m}$ about B through the angle β (where $0 < \beta < 180°$) brings it in the position of $\mathbf{n}$, and this is the case if the vector product $\mathbf{m} \times \mathbf{n}$ is positive. In a right-handed coordinate system, with $\mathbf{m}$ and $\mathbf{n}$ lying in the xy-plane, this vector product has the direction of the z-axis (and its length is $\sin \beta$). More precisely, we have:

$$\mathbf{m} \times \mathbf{n} = s\mathbf{k}$$

where $\mathbf{k}$ is a unit vector in the direction of the positive z-axis, and:

$s = \sin \beta > 0 \quad$ if A, B, C, in that order, are counterclockwise;
$s = -\sin \beta < 0$ if A, B, C, in that order, are clockwise.

With $\mathbf{i}$ and $\mathbf{j}$ as unit vectors in the directions of the positive x- and y-axes, respectively, we can use the 'determinant notation'

$$\mathbf{m} \times \mathbf{n} = \begin{vmatrix} \mathbf{i} & \mathbf{j} & \mathbf{k} \\ m_1 & m_2 & 0 \\ n_1 & n_2 & 0 \end{vmatrix}$$

It follows from this that

$$s = m_1 n_2 - n_1 m_2$$

If s is positive, A, B, C are counterclockwise; otherwise, they are clockwise. You can find more about this in my book *Programming Principles in Computer Graphics*, and, of course, in mathematics textbooks, such as *Advanced Engineering Mathematics*, by E. Kreyszig.

After these mathematical considerations we should pay attention to the way function *sharpjoint* can be used. If we want a sharp joint B of the line segments AB and BC with width w, we write:

```
fatline0(xA, yA, xB, yB, w);
fatline0(xB, yB, xC, yC, w);
sharpjoint(w);
```

Since *sharpjoint* uses some global variables it is particularly important to write these three function calls in the above order. You need not worry about A, B, C being counterclockwise or clockwise: in either case *sharpjoint* performs its task correctly.

Since functions for fat lines may be useful for various purposes, we will add the following text to the graphics module GRASPTC.C, and declare the new functions in GRASPTC.H.

```
static float xA, yA, xB, yB, xC, yC;

void fatline0(float x1, float y1, float x2, float y2, float d)
{ float dx, dy, dxhw, dyhw, factor, r=d/2;
  int points[10];
  dx = x2 - x1; dy = y2 - y1;
  factor = r/sqrt(dx * dx + dy * dy);
  dxhw = dy * factor; /* Delta x for half the width */
  dyhw = dx * factor; /* Delta y for half the width */
  points[0] = IX(x1+dxhw); points[1] = IY(y1-dyhw);
  points[2] = IX(x2+dxhw); points[3] = IY(y2-dyhw);
  points[4] = IX(x2-dxhw); points[5] = IY(y2+dyhw);
```

```
  points[6] = IX(x1-dxhw); points[7] = IY(y1+dyhw);
  points[8] = points[0]; points[9] = points[1];
  fillpoly(5, points);
  xA = xB; yA = yB;
  xB = x1; yB = y1;
  xC = x2; yC = y2;
}

void fatline(float x1, float y1, float x2, float y2, float d)
{ float r=d/2;
  fatline0(x1, y1, x2, y2, d);
  fillcircle_uc(x1, y1, r);
  fillcircle_uc(x2, y2, r);
}

void sharpjoint(float d)
{ float r=d/2, BA, BC, dxBA, dyBA, dxBC, dyBC, s,
        sina, factor, xD, yD, xE, yE, xF, yF, m1,
        m2, n1, n2, rm1, rm2, rn1, rn2;
  int points[10];
  dxBA = xA - xB; dyBA = yA - yB;
  dxBC = xC - xB; dyBC = yC - yB;
  BA = sqrt(dxBA * dxBA + dyBA * dyBA);
  BC = sqrt(dxBC * dxBC + dyBC * dyBC);
  n1 = -dxBA/BA; n2 = -dyBA/BA;
  m1 = -dxBC/BC; m2 = -dyBC/BC;
  s = m1 * n2 - n1 * m2;
  sina = fabs(s);
  factor = r/sina;
  xD = xB + factor * (m1 + n1);
  yD = yB + factor * (m2 + n2);
  rm1 = r * m1; rm2 = r * m2;
  rn1 = r * n1; rn2 = r * n2;
  if (s > 0)
  { xE = xB - rm2; yE = yB + rm1;
    xF = xB + rn2; yF = yB - rn1;
  } else
  { xE = xB + rm2; yE = yB - rm1;
    xF = xB - rn2; yF = yB + rn1;
  }
  points[0] = IX(xB); points[1] = IY(yB);
  points[2] = IX(xF); points[3] = IY(yF);
  points[4] = IX(xD); points[5] = IY(yD);
  points[6] = IX(xE); points[7] = IY(yE);
  points[8] = points[0]; points[9] = points[1];
  fillpoly(5, points);
}
```

We can now use the following demonstration program, which, after linking its object code together with GRASPTC.OBJ, gives the output shown in Fig. 2.17.

```
/* FATDEMO: Demonstration program for fat lines
            in three different styles
*/

#include <stdio.h>
#include <math.h>
#include "grasptc.h"

main()
{ float xP, yP, xQ, yQ, xR, yR, xS, yS, c, c2, d;
  initgr();
  c = x_max/7; c2 = 2*c; d = c/2;
  xP = xS = c; xQ = xR = c2;
  yP = yQ = c; yR = y_max - c;
  yS = 0.5 * (yP + yR);

  fatline0(xP, yP, xQ, yQ, d);
  fatline0(xQ, yQ, xR, yR, d);
  fatline0(xR, yR, xS, yS, d);
  fatline0(xS, yS, xP, yP, d);

  xP += c2; xQ += c2; xR += c2; xS += c2;

  fatline(xP, yP, xQ, yQ, d);
  fatline(xQ, yQ, xR, yR, d);
  fatline(xR, yR, xS, yS, d);
  fatline(xS, yS, xP, yP, d);

  xP += c2; xQ += c2; xR += c2; xS += c2;

  fatline0(xP, yP, xQ, yQ, d);
  fatline0(xQ, yQ, xR, yR, d); sharpjoint(d);
  fatline0(xR, yR, xS, yS, d); sharpjoint(d);
  fatline0(xS, yS, xP, yP, d); sharpjoint(d);
  fatline0(xP, yP, xQ, yQ, d); sharpjoint(d);
  endgr();
}
```

2.9 BUSINESS GRAPHICS

Statistical data are often presented in the form of diagrams in which certain quantities are proportional to shaded areas. There are four Turbo C functions to produce such diagrams easily. These are declared in GRAPHICS.H as follows:

```
void far bar(int left, int top, int right, int bottom);
void far bar3d(int left, int top, int right, int bottom,
                              int depth, int topflag);
void far pieslice(int x, int y, int stangle, int endangle, int radius);
void far sector(int x, int y, int stangle, int endangle,
                          int xradius, int yradius);
```

Program BARS produces the bars shown in Fig. 2.19. The *bar* function fills a rectangle with the current fill pattern and color. It does not draw the sides of that rectangle. If we want the sides to be drawn, we can use *bar3d*, as we will see.

The *bar3d* function draws a three-dimensional vertical bar, the front face of which is filled with the current fill pattern and color. The visible edges of the bar are drawn. The 'depth' of the bar is given as the fifth argument. Each bar can consist of more than one portion. With *topflag* = 1, the top face of the bar portion is drawn, which obviously must be the case only for the highest portion, so for any lower portions we use *topflag* = 0. It will now be clear that we can use *bar3d* with *depth* = 0 (and any value of *topflag*) to obtain a filled rectangle similar to those obtained with the *bar* function, but with the sides drawn.

```
/* BARS: 2D and 3D bars, to be used in business diagrams.
*/
#include "grasptc.h"

main()
{ int w, h, bottom, depth;
  initgr();
  w = X__max/30; /* Horizontal unit */
  h = Y__max/30; /* Vertical unit   */
  bottom = 20 * h; depth = w/2;

  setfillstyle(SLASH_FILL, foregrcolor);
  bar(6*w, 9*h, 8*w, bottom);                  /* Bar 1 */
  bar3d(16*w, 9*h, 18*w, bottom, depth, 1);

  setfillstyle(INTERLEAVE_FILL, foregrcolor);
  bar(8*w, 8*h, 10*w, bottom);                 /* Bar 2 */
  bar3d(18*w, 8*h, 20*w, bottom, depth, 1);
```

```
    setfillstyle(HATCH_FILL, foregrcolor);
    bar(10*w, 10*h, 12*w, bottom);                    /* Bar 3A */
    bar3d(20*w, 10*h, 22*w, bottom, depth, 0);

    setfillstyle(SOLID_FILL, foregrcolor);
    bar(10*w, 5*h, 12*w, 10*h);                       /* Bar 3B */
    bar3d(20*w, 5*h, 22*w, 10*h, depth, 1);

    endgr();
}
```

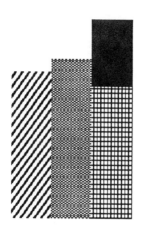 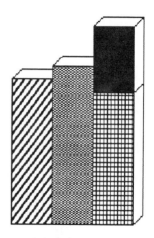

Fig. 2.19. Bars (2D and 3D)

The *pieslice* function draws a filled *sector* of a circle, and *sector* draws a filled elliptic sector. Program SECTORS demonstrates both functions and its output is shown in Fig. 2.20.

```
/* SECTORS: Pieslices and elliptic sectors for business diagrams.
*/
#include "grasptc.h"

main()
{ int XC, YC, XE, YE, R, H;
  initgr();
  XC = X__max/3; XE = 2*X__max/3, R = (XE - XC)/3; H = R/3;
  YC = YE = Y__max/2;
```

```
setfillstyle(SOLID_FILL, foregrcolor);
pieslice(XC, YC, 0, 10, R);                 /* Sector 1 */
sector(XE, YE, 0, 10, R, H);

setfillstyle(HATCH_FILL, foregrcolor);
pieslice(XC, YC, 10, 60, R);                /* Sector 2 */
sector(XE, YE, 10, 60, R, H);

setfillstyle(LTSLASH_FILL, foregrcolor);
pieslice(XC, YC, 60, 190, R);               /* Sector 3 */
sector(XE, YE, 60, 190, R, H);

setfillstyle(WIDE_DOT_FILL, foregrcolor);
pieslice(XC, YC, 190, 360, R);              /* Sector 4 */
sector(XE, YE, 190, 360, R, H);

endgr();
}
```

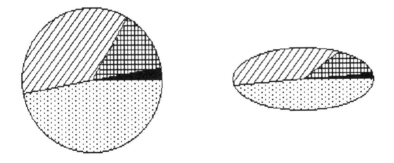

Fig. 2.20. Pieslices and elliptic sectors

CHAPTER 3

Our Final Graphics Product

3.1 INTRODUCTION

It would be of no use if we could display graphics results only on the computer screen. For many years pen plotters were the most common devices for producing line drawings made by computers, but today there is a tendency to use printers instead. Normally a printer is already available for text output, and, if it can also print graphics, we can mix text and graphics before making a hard copy. In addition to a printer we need a *desktop publishing* package to do this. This book is about graphics programming, and in my previous books I have paid no attention to standard software other than DOS and some C compilers. As programmers, we want to deal with source code rather than commercial software packages, which normally are available only in executable form. Adhering to this principle in the extreme would imply dealing with low-level print commands for various printer types and writing all printer software ourselves. You can find an example of such software for nine-pins dot-matrix printers in my book *Computer Graphics for the IBM PC*. Now that both 24-pins and laser printers are becoming increasingly popular, writing basic printer software for a large class of users is no longer an attractive subject for a book such as this. Also it is useless writing software for printing only graphics output if incorporating pictures into text documents is what we really want. Doing this with software written by ourselves means that we would have to write a complete desktop publishing program, which is clearly beyond the scope of this book.

Now that general higher-level tools are widely available, why not use them? Although there are several other good word processors and desktop publishing packages, let us use WordPerfect Version 5.0 as an example. Mentioning the version number is relevant here, because WordPerfect 4.2 was only a word processor, without any graphics facilities, whereas with Version 5.0 we can also do desktop publishing. We can use it to import the graphics results produced by our own programs into a document, and then send it to a printer. I did the typesetting of this book, including the illustrations, in this way, and printed the material on a Hewlett-Packard LaserJet II. If you are familiar with, for example,

Ventura Publisher, WordPerfect may not exactly be what you expect from a desktop publishing package, but, on the other hand, if you already use Word-Perfect to enter the text of your (large) document, it is helpful if, in the final stage, you need not switch to another package to obtain the layout you want. It means that you can use WordPerfect's excellent text-processing facilities, such as search and replace commands and macros, not only in the preparation stage but also later, when you are editing and making corrections.

There are two ways of storing graphics results in files, each with its own positive and negative characteristics. We will distinguish these by the terms *bit-mapped* graphics and *vector* graphics. Let us assume for the moment that such files are available. We then need to know how to use them, and this we will discuss first.

3.2 USING GRAPHICS IN WORDPERFECT 5.0

There are many good books that explain WordPerfect, and this is not intended to be one of them. We will discuss the graphics possibilities of this text processor only as far as we need them for Turbo C graphics. In fact, WordPerfect is very helpful if we know the principle of something but we cannot remember its details. In most cases, we can simply press the 'Help key', that is, function key F3, followed by the first letter of the subject we are interested in, so if this subject happens to be 'graphics' we type F3-G. The screen then says that Alt-F9 is the key combination to be used for graphics. If we use it, a one-line menu is displayed, from which we select

```
1 Figure
```

by pressing 1. This gives rise to another menu, from which we select

```
1 Create
```

Then yet another menu appears, the first option of which is

```
1 - Filename
```

so again we type 1, after which we are requested to enter the name of the graphics file to be imported. We'll discuss shortly how to obtain such files; after importing a graphics file we can modify its size, and, if it is a bit-mapped file, we can invert its pixels, which is highly desirable as a rule. When printing the file on a dot-matrix or a laser printer (using Shift-F7 followed by 1 if we want to print the full document) the picture is printed, along with any text also present in the WordPerfect file. Before printing, it is highly recommended to 'preview' the document, using Shift-F7, followed by 6.

Although WordPerfect is capable of importing many graphics file formats we will use only two, namely .WPG and .HPG formats. They are representative of two distinct classes, *bit-mapped graphics*, discussed in this and the next section, and *vector graphics*, to be dealt with in Section 3.4.

Bit-mapped graphics (.WPG files)

We regard bit-mapped graphics as a collection of pixels on the computer screen. Writing this to a file (and eventually to a printer) implies that all possibilities as regards the shape and appearance of the picture on the screen are also available on the printer. This applies in particular to filled areas, as discussed in Section 2.6.

The drawbacks of bit-mapped graphics are:

- If a line is jagged due to poor resolution, then it will also be jagged on the printer.
- If in WordPerfect we reduce a figure in size, then thin lines may partly disappear.
- The files are in some unknown binary format, so it will be difficult or even impossible to generate them by our own programs.

3.3 THE GRAB UTILITY

The last point of the previous section may disappoint us as programmers, but it is really not as bad as it looks. WordPerfect 5.0 comes with a utility, called GRAB, which enables us to create .WPG files very easily. Before we start our graphics Turbo C program we type

```
GRAB
```

This program then becomes memory resident, and a message on the screen tells us how it should be used. Later, when our program has produced a picture, which is still visible on the screen, we can say that we want to 'capture' it by pressing the keys Shift-Alt-F9. After doing this, a box in the form of a dashed rectangle appears on the screen, denoting the boundaries of the screen area that will actually be captured. We can move or enlarge this box, so as to make sure that everything we are interested in lies inside it. Moving the box in each of the four main directions is done by pressing the arrow keys. We can alter the size of the box by pressing one of these keys while we keep the Shift-key down. For example, if we press the Shift and the Arrow-Right keys simultaneously, the right-hand boundary of the box moves to the right; if we use the Shift and the Arrow-Left keys instead, then that boundary moves to the left. In both cases the effect of keeping the Shift-key down is that the left-hand boundary of the box stays where it is. After the box has the right size and position we have to press the Enter-key. Only then will the actual screen-capture process take place. If we do this the first time, the resulting file will be called GRAB.WPG. If a file with that name already exists, the new file name will be GRAB1.WPG, then GRAB2.WPG, and so on.

Thus creating a .WPG file is quite a simple task. Note that we use GRAB in combination with our own graphics programs, so, unlike graphics programs such as PC Paintbrush and GEM Paint, it does not deprive us of the fun of programming! Another attractive point is that GRAB is available to everyone who works with WordPerfect 5.0 (which is a very popular software package), so it need not be purchased separately.

GRAB gives good results if the picture consists of filled areas, as, for example, Fig. 2.11 in Section 2.6 shows. If we use it for pictures with (thin) lines, these lines may partly disappear if we reduce the scale. After all, a .WPG file consists of a number of pixels, and reducing the scale implies reducing that number of pixels. This applies to all directions, so it may reduce not only the length but also the thickness of a line. Now suppose that we have, for example, a horizontal line with a length of 100 pixels and a width of one pixel. If we reduce it by some factor, say, 0.7, then we can imagine the result to be the product of two operations. First, the line length is reduced in the horizontal direction to 70 pixels, which is what we want, but, second, the image is reduced in the vertical direction, for which we have no possibilities other than the line thicknesses 0 and 1. This means that there is a probability of 70 per cent that the line will remain one pixel wide and a probability of 30 per cent that it will disappear. With vertical lines the situation is similar: scale reduction may cause them to disappear. Sloping lines will have holes after reduction. All this is, of course, not acceptable, so we must not reduce bit-mapped images that contain thin lines but rather ensure that the portion of the screen captured by GRAB is not larger than what we eventually want. We can do this by not using the full screen when we are producing the picture in our program and adjust the box size (discussed above) to the size of the our final product. Another solution is to make all thin lines and curves 'fatter', so that their thickness is at least two pixels. We will discuss this method in more detail in Section 5.4. Fortunately, if our picture consists only of lines (not of filled areas) there is a better option, which we will now discuss.

3.4 HP-GL VECTOR GRAPHICS

With vector graphics a picture is basically a collection of line segments. Only the end points of these line segments need to be known to draw the entire picture. As an extension, it is customary to include also strings of text (with their start positions) as basic items. The main advantage of vector graphics is that the quality of lines does not depend on the resolution of the screen. Thus, lines will improve when sent to a printer with a resolution higher than that of the video screen. If we change the scale of a picture, lines will be only longer or shorter, not thicker or thinner. Pictures with solid-filled areas do not consist of (a finite number of) line segments, so we cannot easily use vector graphics for them. We will not discuss all the formats that can be used for vector graphics but will restrict ourselves to one that is very simple and yet sufficient for our purposes, namely HP-GL, which stands for Hewlett-Packard Graphic Language. (Since DOS file-name extensions consist of, at most, three characters, HP-GL is abbreviated to HPG.) An advantage of .HPG files is that they are in the well-known ASCII format and in codes that we as programmers can easily understand and therefore generate ourselves. HP-GL has originally been designed for plotters. You can find some information about how to use plotters in my book *Interactive 3D Computer Graphics*. This contains a program PLOTHP, which primarily translates coded 'move' and 'draw' operations into the corresponding HP-GL instructions and sends these to a Hewlett-Packard plotter. In that book these coded move- and draw-operations are generated in the functions *move* and *draw* themselves, as a by-product, only if the global variable *fplot*, a file pointer, is not equal to *NULL*. Under the same condition our new versions of *move* and *draw* will do the same, except that they will now directly generate HP-GL instructions, and write them in a file.

In fact, we will use only a small subset of HP-GL. On the one hand, there are some HP-GL instructions (such as one to control the speed of a plotter pen) that we do not need, and, on the other, there are instructions that, although useful, are not supported by WordPerfect 5.0. All the instructions we will be using can be found in the following sample HP-GL program, which gives the result shown in Fig. 3.1.

```
IN;SC0,10000,0,7000;SR2,3.5;DT~;
PU;PA1000,1000;PD;PA9000,1000;
PA1000,6000;PA1000,1000;
PU;PA900,600;LBA~;
PU;PA9050,600;LBB~;
PU;PA950,6050;LBC~;
PU;PA2500,100;LBRight-angled triangle ABC~;
```

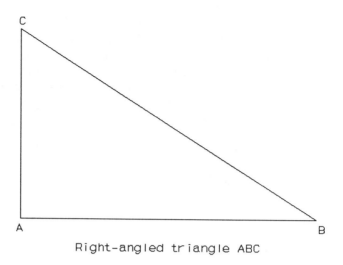

Right-angled triangle ABC

Fig. 3.1. Result of sample HP-GL program

The HP-GL instructions used here have the following meanings:

`IN;`
　　'Initialize.'

`SC0,10000,0,7000;`
　　'Scale.' This instruction says that the allowed minimum and maximum values for x will be 0 and 10 000, respectively. Similarly, the allowed extreme values for y will be 0 and 7 000. In HP-GL, coordinates are integers, so we cannot use our normal user coordinates with maximum values x_max = 10.0 and $y\_max \approx 7.0$. We will therefore multiply those user coordinates by 1000 and round them to the nearest integers.

`SR2,3.5;`
　　'Relative character size.' This instruction sets the character width and height. These are expressed as percentages of the width and the height of the whole drawing. Therefore the width and the height of a character as used here correspond to $2/100 \times 10000 = 200$ horizontal and $3.5/100 \times 7000 = 245$ vertical units specified in the SC instruction.

`DT~;`
　　'Define terminator.' Here the DT instruction says that the character ~ will be used in LB instructions as a terminator for character strings. The default

terminator is the character with ASCII value 3; since not all editors and word processors enable us to type this character easily, it may be preferable to use some visible character such as ~ in HP-GL programs that we write ourselves, accepting that this makes it impossible to use this character inside a string in the normal way. For this reason, we will not use the DT instruction when generating HP-GL in our C programs but rather use the default terminator, written in C as '\003'.

`PU;`

'Pen Up.'

`PD;`

'Pen Down.'

`PA1000,1000;`

'Plot Absolute.' Depending on the position of the pen (Up or Down), the pen only moves to the given point above the paper surface or it moves the pen from the current position to that point while touching the paper, so that a (straight) line segment is drawn.

`LBA~;`

'Label.' All characters between LB and the terminating character (~) are drawn horizontally, starting at the current position, given by a previous PA instruction. In fact that point will lie a little below the lower-left corner of the first character: if we draw both a horizontal line and a string using the same y-coordinate the string will be appear a little above that line. The character width and height will be used as specified in the SR instruction.

3.5 GENERATING HP-GL INSTRUCTIONS

Lines

We will now extend our graphics module GRASPTC so that it can automatically generate HP-GL instructions that correspond to what we see on the screen. Remember that this graphics module is intended to be used by problem-oriented programmers, who are primarily interested in the mathematical or technical aspects of their own programming problems and who therefore do not want to spend time in dealing with the peculiarities of operating systems, graphics adapters, and compilers. This does not necessarily mean that GRASPTC users are beginners in the art of C programming. The C language is not a very complex one to learn, and there are very few superfluous language constructs, if any. I therefore hope that you are familiar with the concept of file pointers, such as *fplot*, defined in GRASPTC.C as follows:

```
#include <stdio.h>
FILE *fplot=NULL;
```

The header file GRASPTC.H, which we will always include in our graphics programs by means of the line

```
#include "grasptc.h"
```

contains the following declaration of *fplot*:

```
extern FILE *fplot;
```

This means that, apart from including GRASPTC.H, we need not declare this file pointer in our own program if we want to use it. Now the important thing to remember is that an HP-GL file is automatically obtained by using our familiar functions *initgr*, *move*, and *draw*, if, before calling *initgr*, we change *fplot*'s default value, *NULL*, into a real file pointer by writing, for example,

```
fplot = fopen("figure.hpg", "w");
```

Although you need not really know how *fplot* is used in GRASPTC, we will discuss this, for it is instructive and very simple. The following if-statement is inserted in *initgr*, after the computation of *y_max*:

```
if (fplot != NULL)
   fprintf(fplot, "IN;SC0,10000,0,%d;\n", plotcoor(y_max));
```

Thus, HP-GL instructions are written in the file supplied by the user through the variable *fplot* if he or she has done so. If not, no HP-GL instructions are written, and *initgr* works as previously.

In the last program line the macro *plotcoor* is used. It computes plot coordinates and is defined as follows:

```
#define plotcoor(x) ((int)(1000 * (x) + 0.5))
```

Then the following if-statement is inserted in the function *move*:

```
if (fplot != NULL)
   fprintf(fplot, "PU;PA%d,%d;", plotcoor(x), plotcoor(y));
```

Similarly, the function *draw* contains the statement:

```
if (fplot != NULL)
   fprintf(fplot, "PD;PA%d,%d;", plotcoor(x), plotcoor(y));
```

Text

If *fplot* is not equal to *NULL*, we also want to write HP-GL instructions for text to the output file, accessible through *fplot*. But with text, things are slightly more complex. The Turbo C functions *outtext* and *outtextxy*, discussed in Section 1.6, are based on the convention that by default the start point lies in the upper-left corner of the first character, while HP-GL places the text such that the current position will lie somewhat below the lower-left corner. In addition, Turbo C lets us choose among various fonts and character sizes; when using HP-GL, the only font supported by WordPerfect is 'Helvetica', which corresponds more or less to sansserif font in Turbo C. We will now add the function *grtext* to GRASPTC to obtain text both on the screen and in an HP-GL file at the same time. Called in the graphics mode, it displays a character string, and, if *fplot* has a value other than *NULL*, it also writes the corresponding string to an HP-GL file. The arguments of *grtext* are based on HP-GL, so we use the lower-left corner of the first character.

Its arguments are such that they can be used without conversion for the generation of HP-GL instructions; they are then converted to arguments required by the Turbo C graphics functions. Especially with regard to character size, the text written by *grtext* on the screen is only an approximation of that in the HP-GL file, which will eventually be printed and should therefore be considered more important.

Before discussing how *grtext* works let us see how to use this function. This is declared in GRASPTC.H as follows:

```
void grtext(float xleft, float ylower, float heightpercent, char *str);
```

Its first two arguments denote the start point of the text in the sense of HP-GL: the lower-left corner of the first character will lie a little above that point. The third argument, *heightpercent*, is the character height, expressed as a percentage of the total height of the picture. The string to be displayed and drawn is given by the fourth argument, *str*. Function *grtext* itself places the terminator ('\003') at the end of the string, so the user can simply write strings in the normal way. Program HPGLTEXT shows how the text

```
ABCabc
```

will appear in with the height percentages

2, 4, ..., 16

It also draws horizontal lines with the same y-coordinates as those used for the text.

```
/* HPGLTEXT: Test program for text in HP-GL
*/
#include "grasptc.h"
main()
{ float x=1.0, y, h_perc;
  fplot = fopen("test.hpg", "w");
  initgr();
  y = 0.1;
  for (h_perc=2.0; h_perc<17; h_perc+=2.0)
  { grtext(x, y, h_perc, "ABCabc");
    move(x, y); draw(8.0, y);
    y += h_perc/100.0 * y_max + 0.2;
  }
  endgr();
}
```

If we run program HPGLTEXT, the result on the screen is as shown in Fig. 3.2.

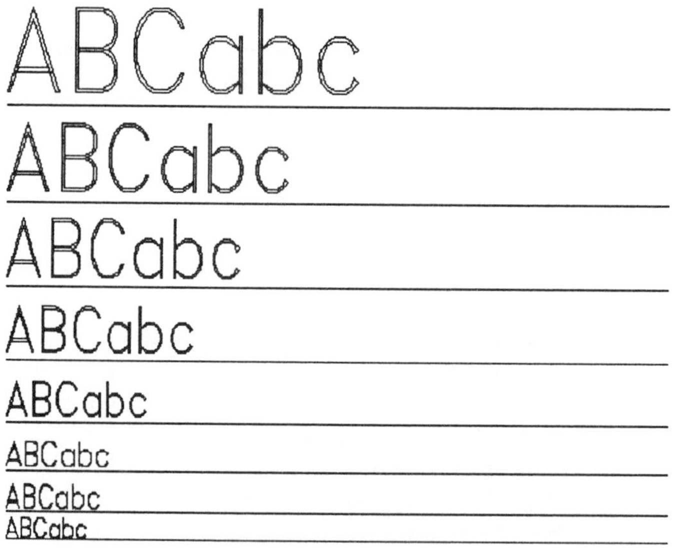

Fig. 3.2. Output of HPGLTEXT on-screen

To obtain Fig. 3.2 as hard copy I have used the Grab utility, discussed in Section 3.3. After importing the file GRAB.WPG in WordPerfect, it was necessary to invert all pixels, using

```
Alt-F9
Figure (1)
Edit (2)
Figure number (...)
Edit (8)
Invert (4)
```

By using the standard C function *fopen* in program HPGLTEXT and assigning its returned value to the external variable *fplot*, the new function *grtext* also writes HP-GL instructions to a file, and so do the functions *initgr*, *move*, and *draw*. This file, TEST.HPG (whose name is given in the call to *fopen*), will have the following contents:

```
IN;SCO,10000,0,6435;
SR1.1,2.0;PU;PA1000,100;LBABCabc^C;
PU;PA1000,100;PD;PA8000,100;
SR2.3,4.0;PU;PA1000,429;LBABCabc^C;
PU;PA1000,429;PD;PA8000,429;
SR3.4,6.0;PU;PA1000,886;LBABCabc^C;
PU;PA1000,886;PD;PA8000,886;
SR4.6,8.0;PU;PA1000,1472;LBABCabc^C;
PU;PA1000,1472;PD;PA8000,1472;
SR5.7,10.0;PU;PA1000,2187;LBABCabc^C;
PU;PA1000,2187;PD;PA8000,2187;
SR6.9,12.0;PU;PA1000,3030;LBABCabc^C;
PU;PA1000,3030;PD;PA8000,3030;
SR8.0,14.0;PU;PA1000,4003;LBABCabc^C;
PU;PA1000,4003;PD;PA8000,4003;
SR9.1,16.0;PU;PA1000,5104;LBABCabc^C;
PU;PA1000,5104;PD;PA8000,5104;
```

As discussed in Section 2.1, the value of y_max depends on the graphics adapter we have. For HGA, we have $y\_max = 6.435$, which explains the value 6435 in the first line of file TEST.HPG. The notation $^\wedge C$ is used here to denote the end code '\003', at the end of strings in LB instructions. File TEST.HPG is only 569 bytes long, compared with 5877 bytes of the corresponding bit-mapped file, GRAB.WPG. When imported into WordPerfect, it gives the result shown in Fig. 3.3.

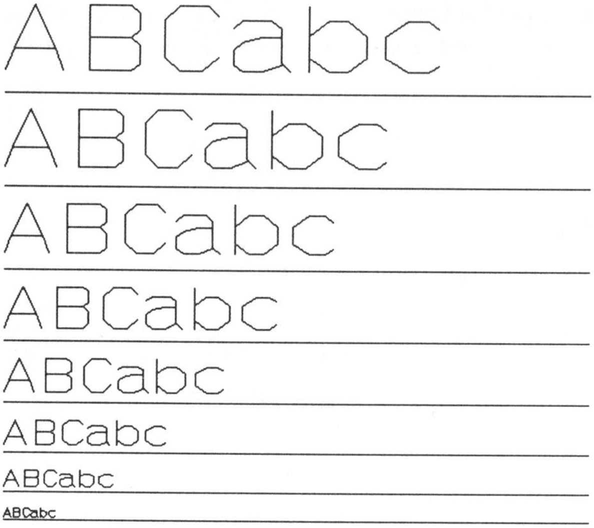

Fig. 3.3. Output of program HPGLTEXT using file TEST.HPG

It is interesting to note the differences between Figs 3.2 and 3.3. Curiously, the sans-serif font of Fig. 3.2 is not really a bit-mapped but rather a 'stroked' font in Turbo C. It is really drawn as straight line segments, and on the screen it looks attractive. Only when we capture the screen do we obtain a bit-mapped file. The contents of this file depends on the resolution of the video display, and we must be careful in altering the size of the image. In Fig. 3.3, however, the lines of which the characters consist are still real lines in the HP-GL file, as it were; only at the very last moment, when sending the image to the printer, are these lines converted to the dots used by the printer.

Now that we have been using *grtext*, it is time to see how this function works. As you can see, the given string *str* is copied to the local string *s*, which is long enough to insert the usual HP-GL end code, '\003', just before the terminating null character, '\0'. As you know, *str* is only the begin address of the actual given character sequence, and we are not entitled to change the characters of that sequence in memory, let alone its length. The constant 4.0/7.0 has been found empirically. You can, of course, change it a little: the larger it is, the wider the characters resulting from the HP-GL file will be.

```
void grtext(float xleft, float ylower, float heightpercent, char *str)
{ char *s;
  int len, charsize;
  float widthpercent=heightpercent*4.0/7.0;
```

```
  len = strlen(str);
  s = farmalloc(len+2);
  if (s == NULL){to_text(); printf("farmalloc");exit(1);}
  strcpy(s, str);
  s[len] = '\003'; s[len+1] = '\0';
  if (fplot != NULL)
  { fprintf(fplot, "SR%3.1f,%3.1f;", widthpercent, heightpercent);
    fprintf(fplot, "PU;PA%d,%d;LB%s;\n",
    plotcoor(xleft), plotcoor(ylower), s);
  }
  charsize = (int)(heightpercent/2 + 0.5);
  if (charsize > 10) charsize = 10;
  settextstyle(SANS_SERIF_FONT, HORIZ_DIR,
  charsize);
  outtextxy(IX(xleft), IY(ylower)-textheight(str)-charsize, str);
  farfree(s);
}
```

3.6 MODULE GRASPTC

Before dealing with the functions of GRASPTC themselves, we will consider
their declarations (also called 'function prototypes') in the header file
GRASPTC.H. Including this file in your graphics programs by means of the line

```
#include "grasptc.h"
```

is highly recommended. I will use this opportunity to summarize our discussions
of the first three chapters of this book, as far as our 'toolbox' GRASPTC is
concerned, and I will do this in the form of comments. If you want to use a
function defined in GRASPTC you will need both a function prototype for
information about the argument types and a brief description about what the
function does. Both elements are available in the following header file:

```
/* GRASPTC.H: Header file, to be used in any module that uses
              the functions defined in GRASPTC.
*/
#ifndef __HUGE__
#error Use Huge Memory Model
#endif
#include <stdio.h>
#include <graphics.h>

extern FILE *fplot;
/* If we assign a value to 'fplot', using fopen(), subsequent
   calls to initgr(), move(), draw(), grtext(), arc_uc(),
   circle80_pc(), circle80_uc(), drawarc3(), and fillet() will
```

```
   cause HP-GL instructions to be written to the stream 'fplot'.
*/


extern int X__max, Y__max, foregrcolor, backgrcolor, colorsum;
/* After initgr() has been called, these variables indicate the
   maximum pixel coordinates X and Y, the foreground and background
   colors, and the sum of these two color codes. The upper-left
   corner of the screen is the origin of the pixel-coordinate system.
*/


extern float x_max, y_max, horfact, vertfact;
/* After initgr() has been called, x_max and y_max denote the maximum
   user coordinates (with x_max = 10.0), and horfact = X__max/x_max,
   vertfact = Y__max/y_max.
   The lower-left corner of the screen is the origin of the user-
   coordinate system.
*/


void initgr(void);
/* Detects the graphics adapter, and switches to the graphics mode
   that has the highest resolution.
*/


void boundaries_uc(void);
/* If the value x_max = 10.0 should be unacceptable to you, you
   can assign a different value to x_max. You can do this only after
   calling initgr(); after such an assignment a call to boundaries_uc
   takes care that the variables y_max, horfact, and vertfact are
   updated accordingly.
*/


int IX(float x);
int IY(float y);
/* Conversion from user to pixel coordinates */

void move(float x, float y);
void draw(float x, float y);
/* The arguments x and y are the user coordinates of the new
   current position. In case of draw(), a straight line is drawn
   from the previous to the new current position.
*/


void endgr(void);
void to_text(void);
/* These two function switch back to text mode. They differ in that
   to_text() does this immediately, while endgr() waits until a
   key is pressed.
*/
```

```c
void invertpixel(int X, int Y);
/* Changes pixel (X, Y) (given in pixel coordinates) from background
   to foreground color and vice versa.
*/

void grtext(float xleft, float ylower, float heightpercent, char *str);
/* Writes the string 'str' while in graphics mode. Point (xleft, ylower),
   given in user coordinates, is the lower-left corner of the first
   character. The character height is approximately equal to
   'heightpercent' per cent of the screen height. The string is written
   horizontally, and the font is 'sans serif'.
*/

void circle_uc(float x, float y, float r);
/* Draws a circle, with center (x, y) and radius r given in
   user coordinates.
*/

int XPIX(float xdim);
int YPIX(float ydim);
/* These functions convert distances in user coordinates into distances
   in pixel coordinates.
*/

#define PI 3.141592653589793
void line_uc(float x1, float y1, float x2, float y2);
/* Draws a line between (x1, y1) and (x2, y2). The arguments are
   user coordinates.
*/

void arc_uc(float xC, float yC, float stangle,
            float endangle, float radius, int nlinesegments);
/* Draws a circular arc, with a given center, start angle,
   end angle, and radius, given in user coordinates and radians.
   The arc is approximated by as many line segments as the final
   argument indicates.
*/

struct arc_uctype
{ float x, y, xstart, ystart, xend, yend;
};
/* Type definition which enables us to use type 'struct arc_uctype'
   to define (and declare) variables; the address of such a variable
   can be used as an argument of function getarc_uc().
*/

void getarc_uc(struct arc_uctype *arccoords);
/* After a call to arc_uc() or fillet(), function getarc_uc() places
```

```
   the (user) coordinates of the center, the start point, and the end
   point of the arc in the structure pointed to by 'arccoords'.
*/


float angle(float x, float y);
/* Returns the angle (-PI/2 < angle <= 3*PI/2) between the positive
   x-axis and the line through the origin O and point (x, y).
*/


float drawarc3(float xA, float yA, float xB, float yB,
               float xC, float yC, float *pr);
/* Draws an arc that connects the points (xA, yA) and (xC, yC),
   and that passes through point (xB, yB). The radius of the arc
   is placed in the variable pointed to by 'pr'. The arguments
   are in user coordinates. The function returns a positive
   value if the points A, B, C, in that order, are counter-
   clockwise, and a negative value if they are clockwise.
   If A, B, and C are on a straight line, the returned value
   is zero and nothing is drawn.
*/


float fillet(float xA, float yA, float xB, float yB,
             float xC, float yC, float r);
/* Instead of the angle formed by the line segments AB and BC, an
   arc with radius r and tangent to these line segments is drawn.
   The arc can be used as a rounded corner B. The start and end
   points of the arc can be obtained by calling getarc_uc(). All
   arguments are in user coordinates. Returned value: see drawarc3().
*/


void fillcircle_uc(float x, float y, float radius);
/* Draws a filled circle, with center and radius given in
   user coordinates. A call to this function should be preceded
   by a call to the Turbo C function setfillstyle() to set the
   fill style and fill pattern.
*/


void circle80_pc(int XC, int YC, int R);
/* Draws a circle approximated by 80 line segments. In contrast to
   the Turbo C function circle(), circle80_pc() inverts pixels after
   the call setwritemode(XOR_PUT). Also, the 80 line segments are
   written in an HP-GL file if 'fplot' is not equal to NULL.
   The arguments are pixel coordinates.
*/


void circle80_uc(float xC, float yC, float r);
/* Similar to circle80(), but with arguments in user coordinates.
*/
```

```
void fatline0(float x1, float y1, float x2, float y2, float d);
/* Draws a fat line with thickness d between the end points
   (x1, y1) and (x2, y2). In fact a filled rectangle is drawn
   with the given end points as midpoints of two opposite sides.
   The arguments are in user coordinates. See also fatline() and
   sharpjoint().
*/

void fatline(float x1, float y1,  float x2, float y2, float d);
/* As fatline0(), but now two filled circles with the end points as
   centers and d/2 as their radius are also drawn.
*/

void sharpjoint(float d);
/* After the three calls:
     fatline0(xP, yP, xQ, yQ, d);
     fatline0(xQ, yQ, xR, yR, d);
     sharpjoint(d);
   there will be a sharp angle at Q, the point of intersection.
*/
```

Special attention should be paid to the following lines, which occur at the beginning of GRASPTC.H:

```
#ifndef __HUGE__
#error Use Huge Memory Model
#endif
```

These make the compiler check whether the huge memory model is used. If it is not, the error message

```
Use Huge Memory Model
```

is displayed. Since we will use the line

```
#include "grasptc.h"
```

in all our graphics programs, this message will appear whenever the current memory model is wrong. Recall that you can change this in the Turbo C integrated environment by selecting Options, Compiler, Model, Huge, and don't forget to store these options.

Note that GRASPTC.H also contains the line

```
#include <graphics.h>
```

Thus, declaring our functions by means of the header file GRASPTC.H implies that all Turbo C graphics functions and symbolic constants are also declared.

We now turn to the file GRASPTC.C. This contains some additions and enhancements to what we have discussed so far. There are two functions, _graphgetmem_ and _graphfreemem_, that we will not use ourselves, nor are they used by other functions in GRASPTC. In the Turbo C Reference Manual they are called 'user hooks'. They are used by routines in the Turbo C graphics library, instead of default versions, which call *malloc* and *free* to allocate and release memory for buffers, etc. As our versions call *farmalloc* and *farfree* instead we avoid any problems that may arise as a result of the 64K limitation that applies to *malloc*.

Routines and variables in GRASPTC that are only for internal use are given the *static* attribute. They are not published to the linker and therefore cannot be used in our own program modules. All other functions in GRASPTC have been discussed in this and the preceding chapters.

```c
/* GRASPTC: Graphics System for Programming in Turbo C.
*/
#include <dos.h>
#include <stdio.h>
#include <graphics.h>
#include <conio.h>
#include <math.h>
#include <stdlib.h>
#include <alloc.h>
#include <string.h>
#include "grasptc.h"

/* Functions to install the break handler for graphics mode: */
#define CTRL_C 0x2E03
#define CTRL_BREAK 0x8000
static void interrupt (*oldInt9)(void);
static int *keybuffer  = (int *)0x41E;
static int *buffertail = (int *)0x41C;
static int handler_installed = 0;

static void restore_old_break(void)
{ if (handler_installed)
  { setvect(9, oldInt9); handler_installed = 0;
  }
}

static void interrupt newInt9(void)
{ unsigned int tail, code;
  oldInt9();
```

```
  /* *buffertail = 30, 32, ..., 60 */
  tail = (*buffertail - 30) >> 1;
  /* tail = 0, 1, ..., 15 */
  code = keybuffer[tail ? tail - 1 : 15];
  if (code == CTRL_C || code == CTRL_BREAK)
  { to_text();
    exit(1);
  }
}

static void installBreak(void)
{ if (!handler_installed)
  { oldInt9 = getvect(9); setvect(9,newInt9);
    handler_installed = 1;
  }
}

#define plotcoor(x) ((int)(1000 * (x) + 0.5))

int X__max, Y__max, foregrcolor, backgrcolor, colorsum;
static int Xcur, Ycur;
float x_max, y_max, horfact, vertfact;
FILE *fplot=NULL;


void boundaries_uc(void)
{ int w, h;
  getaspectratio(&w, &h);
  y_max = x_max * (float)Y__max*h/((float)X__max*w);
  horfact = X__max/x_max; vertfact = Y__max/y_max;
}

void initgr(void)
{ int gdriver=DETECT, gmode;
  /* The following calls to registerfarbgidriver() and
     registerfarbgifont() assume that you have created the
     object files CGAF.OBJ, EGAVGAF.OBJ, HERCF.OBJ,
     TRIPF.OBJ, LITTF.OBJ, SANSF.OBJ, using the commands
     BGIOBJ /F CGA, BGIOBJ /F EGAVGA, and so on. You can omit
     some of these calls or insert others as you like, see
     also Section 1.7.
  */
  registerfarbgidriver(CGA_driver_far);
  registerfarbgidriver(EGAVGA_driver_far);
  registerfarbgidriver(Herc_driver_far);
  registerfarbgifont(triplex_font_far);
  registerfarbgifont(small_font_far);
  registerfarbgifont(sansserif_font_far);
```

```
   initgraph(&gdriver, &gmode, "\\tc");
   /* Third argument "\\tc" will normally not be used! */
   if (graphresult())
   { printf("\nGraphics driver not available.\n"); exit(1);
   }
   installBreak();
   foregrcolor = getcolor(); backgrcolor = getbkcolor();
   colorsum = foregrcolor + backgrcolor;
   X__max = getmaxx(); Y__max = getmaxy();
   x_max=10.0;
   boundaries_uc();
   if (fplot != NULL)
      fprintf(fplot, "IN;SC0,10000,0,%d;\n", plotcoor(y_max));
}

void invertpixel(int X, int Y)
{ putpixel(X, Y, colorsum - getpixel(X, Y));
}

int IX(float x)
{ return (int) (x * horfact + 0.5);
}

int IY(float y)
{ return Y__max - (int)(y * vertfact + 0.5);
}

void move(float x, float y)
{ Xcur = IX(x); Ycur = IY(y);
  moveto(Xcur, Ycur);
  if (fplot != NULL) fprintf(fplot, "PU;PA%d,%d;",
  plotcoor(x), plotcoor(y));
}

void draw(float x, float y)
{ int X0=Xcur, Y0=Ycur;
  Xcur = IX(x); Ycur = IY(y);
  line(X0, Y0, Xcur, Ycur);
  moveto(Xcur, Ycur);
  if (fplot != NULL) fprintf(fplot, "PD;PA%d,%d;\n",
  plotcoor(x), plotcoor(y));
}

void to_text(void)
{ closegraph();
  restore_old_break();
}
```

```c
void endgr(void)
{ getch(); to_text();
}

void grtext(float xleft, float ylower, float heightpercent, char *str)
{ char *s;
  int len, charsize;
  float widthpercent=heightpercent*4.0/7.0;
  len = strlen(str);
  s = farmalloc(len+2);
  if (s == NULL){to_text(); printf("farmalloc");exit(1);}
  strcpy(s, str);
  s[len] = '\003'; s[len+1] = '\0';
  if (fplot != NULL)
  { fprintf(fplot, "SR%3.1f,%3.1f;",
    widthpercent, heightpercent);
    fprintf(fplot, "PU;PA%d,%d;LB%s;\n",
    plotcoor(xleft), plotcoor(ylower), s);
  }
  charsize = (int)(heightpercent/2 + 0.5);
  if (charsize > 10) charsize = 10;
  settextstyle(SANS_SERIF_FONT, HORIZ_DIR, charsize);
  outtextxy(IX(xleft), IY(ylower)-textheight(str)-charsize, str);
  farfree(s);
}

void far * far _graphgetmem(unsigned size)
{ char far *p;
  p = farmalloc((long)size);
  if (p == NULL) {printf("Mem. space in _graphgetmem"); exit(1);}
  return p;
}

void far _graphfreemem(void far *ptr, unsigned size)
{ farfree(ptr);
}

void line_uc(float x1, float y1, float x2, float y2)
{ line(IX(x1), IY(y1), IX(x2), IY(y2));
}

void circle_uc(float x, float y, float r)
{ circle(IX(x), IY(y), IX(r));
}

int XPIX(float xdim)
{ return (int)(xdim * horfact + 0.5);
}
```

```
int YPIX(float ydim)
{ return (int)(ydim * vertfact + 0.5);
}


static float xarc_C, yarc_C, xarc_start, yarc_start, xarc_end, yarc_end;

void arc_uc(float xC, float yC, float stangle,
            float endangle, float radius, int nlinesegments)
{ float theta, phi;
  int i;
  while (endangle < stangle) endangle += 2*PI;
  theta = (endangle - stangle)/nlinesegments;
  xarc_start = xC + radius*cos(stangle);
  yarc_start = yC + radius*sin(stangle);
  xarc_end = xC + radius*cos(endangle);
  yarc_end = yC + radius*sin(endangle);
  move(xarc_start, yarc_start);
  for (i=1; i<nlinesegments; i++)
  { phi = stangle + i * theta;
    draw(xC+radius*cos(phi), yC+radius*sin(phi));
  }
  draw(xarc_end, yarc_end);
  xarc_C = xC; yarc_C = yC;
}


void getarc_uc(struct arc_uctype *arccoords)
{ arccoords->x = xarc_C;
  arccoords->y = yarc_C;
  arccoords->xstart = xarc_start;
  arccoords->ystart = yarc_start;
  arccoords->xend = xarc_end;
  arccoords->yend = yarc_end;
}


float angle(float x, float y)
{ return (x > 0 ? atan(y/x) :
         x < 0 ? PI + atan(y/x) :
         y >= 0 ? PI/2 : 3*PI/2);
}


float drawarc3(float xA, float yA,
            float xB, float yB,
            float xC, float yC,
            float *pr)
{ float u1, u2, n1, n2, xD, yD, v1, v2, m1, m2, xE, yE, lambda,
    xO, yO, r1, r2, r, stangle, endangle, phiA, phiC, determinant;
  int nsteps;
  u1 = xB - xA; u2 = yB - yA; /* Vector u points from A to B    */
```

```
    n1 = u2; n2 = -u1;              /* Vector n is perpendicular to u */
    xD = (xA+xB)/2; yD = (yA+yB)/2;         /* D is midpoint of AB */

    v1 = xC - xB; v2 = yC - yB; /* Vector v points from B to C    */
    m1 = v2; m2 = -v1;              /* Vector m is perpendicular to v */
    xE = (xB+xC)/2; yE = (yB+yC)/2;         /* E is midpoint of BC */
    determinant = m2*n1 - m1*n2;
    if (determinant == 0.0) return 0.0;
    lambda = (m2*(xE-xD) - m1*(yE-yD))/determinant;
                            /* Vector lambda.n points from D to O */
    xO = xD + lambda * n1;   /* O is center of circle through    */
    yO = yD + lambda * n2;   /* A, B, and C.                     */
    r1 = xA-xO; r2 = yA-yO; /* Vector (r1, r2) points from O to A */
    r = sqrt(r1*r1 + r2*r2);
    phiA = angle(r1, r2);
    phiC = angle(xC-xO, yC-yO);
    if (determinant > 0)
    { stangle = phiA; endangle = phiC;
    } else
    { stangle = phiC; endangle = phiA;
    }
    if (endangle < stangle) endangle += 2*PI;
    nsteps = (int)(r * (endangle - stangle) * 10) + 1;
      /* Number of steps dependent on both radius and angle */
    arc_uc(xO, yO, stangle, endangle, r, nsteps);
    *pr = r;
    return determinant;
}


float fillet(float xA, float yA, float xB, float yB,
             float xC, float yC, float r)
{ float n1, n2, m1, m2, BA, BC, s1, s2, length_of_s,
    b1, b2, cosa, sina, BO1, BO2, xO, yO, proj,
    xD, yD, xE, yE, xF, yF, q;
  n1 = xA - xB; n2 = yA - yB;
  BA = sqrt(n1*n1 + n2*n2);
  n1 /= BA; n2 /= BA;

  m1 = xC - xB; m2 = yC - yB;
  BC = sqrt(m1*m1 + m2*m2);
  m1 /= BC; m2 /= BC;

  s1 = n1 + m1; s2 = n2 + m2;
  length_of_s = sqrt(s1*s1 + s2*s2);
  b1 = s1/length_of_s; b2 = s2/length_of_s;
  cosa = length_of_s/2;
  sina = sqrt(1 - cosa*cosa); q = r/sina;
  BO1 = q * b1; BO2 = q * b2;
```

```
    xO = xB + BO1; yO = yB + BO2;
    proj = BO1 * n1 + BO2 * n2;
    xD = xB + proj * n1; yD = yB + proj * n2;
    xE = xB + proj * m1; yE = yB + proj * m2;
    xF = xO - r * b1; yF = yO - r * b2;
    return drawarc3(xD, yD, xF, yF, xE, yE, &r);
}


void fillcircle_uc(float x, float y, float radius)
{ fillellipse(IX(x), IY(y), XPIX(radius), YPIX(radius));
}


#define COSDELTA 0.996917333733
#define SINDELTA 0.078459095728

void circle80_pc(int XC, int YC, int R)
/* Circle, approximated by regular 80-gon,
   based on pixel coordinates
*/
{ static int first=1, stdpoints[162];
  int j=0, H, V, points[162];
  double costh, sinth, c0, s0;
  float x, y;
  if (first)
  { first = 0;
    costh = 1.0; sinth = 0.0;
    for (j=0; j<=40; j+=2)
    { H = (int)(1e4 * costh + 0.5);
      V = (int)(1e4 * sinth * vertfact/horfact + 0.5);
      stdpoints[j] = H; stdpoints[j+1] = V;
      if (j)
      { stdpoints[160-j] = H;
        stdpoints[161-j] = -V;
      }
      if (j != 40)
      { stdpoints[80-j] = -H; stdpoints[81-j] = V;
        if (j)
        { stdpoints[80+j] = -H;
          stdpoints[81+j] = -V;
        }
      }
      c0 = costh; s0 = sinth;
      costh = c0 * COSDELTA - s0 * SINDELTA;
      sinth = s0 * COSDELTA + c0 * SINDELTA;
    }
    stdpoints[160] = stdpoints[0];
    stdpoints[161] = stdpoints[1];
  }
```

```c
  for (j=0; j<=160; j+=2)
  { points[j] = XC + (int)(stdpoints[j]*(long)R/10000L);
    points[j+1] = YC + (int)(stdpoints[j+1]*(long)R/10000L);
    if (j) invertpixel(points[j], points[j+1]);
    /* Necessary in case of XOR_PUT */
  }
  if (fplot == NULL) drawpoly(81, points); else
  { for (j=0; j<=80; j++)
    { x = points[2*j]/horfact;
      y = (Y_max - points[2*j+1])/vertfact;
      if (j==0) move(x, y); else draw(x, y);
    }
  }
}


void circle80_uc(float xC, float yC, float r)
/* Circle, approximated by regular 80-gon,
   based on user coordinates
*/
{ circle80_pc(IX(xC), IY(yC), XPIX(r));
}


static float xA, yA, xB, yB, xC, yC;

void fatline0(float x1, float y1, float x2, float y2, float d)
{ float dx, dy, dxhw, dyhw, factor, r=d/2;
  int points[10];
  dx = x2 - x1; dy = y2 - y1;
  factor = r/sqrt(dx * dx + dy * dy);
  dxhw = dy * factor;  /* Delta x for half the width */
  dyhw = dx * factor;  /* Delta y for half the width */
  points[0] = IX(x1+dxhw); points[1] = IY(y1-dyhw);
  points[2] = IX(x2+dxhw); points[3] = IY(y2-dyhw);
  points[4] = IX(x2-dxhw); points[5] = IY(y2+dyhw);
  points[6] = IX(x1-dxhw); points[7] = IY(y1+dyhw);
  points[8] = points[0]; points[9] = points[1];
  fillpoly(5, points);
  xA = xB; yA = yB;
  xB = x1; yB = y1;
  xC = x2; yC = y2;
}


void fatline(float x1, float y1, float x2, float y2, float d)
{ float r=d/2;
  fatline0(x1, y1, x2, y2, d);
  fillcircle_uc(x1, y1, r);
  fillcircle_uc(x2, y2, r);
}
```

```
void sharpjoint(float d)
{ float r=d/2, BA, BC, dxBA, dyBA, dxBC, dyBC, s,
        sina, factor, xD, yD, xE, yE, xF, yF, m1,
        m2, n1, n2, rm1, rm2, rn1, rn2;
  int points[10];
  dxBA = xA - xB; dyBA = yA - yB;
  dxBC = xC - xB; dyBC = yC - yB;
  BA = sqrt(dxBA * dxBA + dyBA * dyBA);
  BC = sqrt(dxBC * dxBC + dyBC * dyBC);
  n1 = -dxBA/BA; n2 = -dyBA/BA;
  m1 = -dxBC/BC; m2 = -dyBC/BC;
  s = m1 * n2 - n1 * m2;
  sina = fabs(s);
  factor = r/sina;
  xD = xB + factor * (m1 + n1);
  yD = yB + factor * (m2 + n2);
  rm1 = r * m1; rm2 = r * m2;
  rn1 = r * n1; rn2 = r * n2;
  if (s > 0)
  { xE = xB - rm2; yE = yB + rm1;
    xF = xB + rn2; yF = yB - rn1;
  } else
  { xE = xB + rm2; yE = yB - rm1;
    xF = xB - rn2; yF = yB + rn1;
  }
  points[0] = IX(xB); points[1] = IY(yB);
  points[2] = IX(xF); points[3] = IY(yF);
  points[4] = IX(xD); points[5] = IY(yD);
  points[6] = IX(xE); points[7] = IY(yE);
  points[8] = points[0]; points[9] = points[1];
  fillpoly(5, points);
}
```

CHAPTER 4

Recursion and Fractals

4.1 RECURSION

We say that a function is *recursive* (and that it is based on *recursion*) if that function contains one or more calls to itself or to other functions which in turn call the function under discussion. If a non-recursive function is entered, it is always left before it is entered again, but for a recursive function this need not be the case.

We begin with the very simple triangle of our programs TRIA and TRIA1 of Sections 1.2 and 1.5. In program TRIANGLES we draw such a triangle, but then we call the function *tria*, which connects the midpoints of its sides, so that there will be four smaller triangles. Then *tria* calls itself three times, with the coordinates of the vertices of smaller triangles as arguments. There is also an integer argument, n, which is the *recursion depth*. Starting with some n given by the user, say, 7, that argument is $n - 1$ in each of the three recursive calls, so that 'when we are deepest in the recursion', the value of n is zero, which causes the function to return immediately to its caller, that is, to the function *tria* itself. Note that in program TRIANGLES we can use x_max and y_max even without declaring them explicitly, because they are declared in the header file GRASPTC.H. Figure 4.1 shows the result.

```
/* TRIANGLES: Similar right-angled triangles of various sizes.
*/
#include <stdio.h>
#include "grasptc.h"

void tria(float xA, float yA,    float xB, float yB,
   float xC, float yC, int n)
{ float xP, yP, xQ, yQ, xR, yR;
   if (n > 0)
   { xP = (xB + xC)/2; yP = (yB + yC)/2;
     xQ = (xC + xA)/2; yQ = (yC + yA)/2;
     xR = (xA + xB)/2; yR = (yA + yB)/2;
```

```
      move(xP, yP); draw(xQ, yQ);
      draw(xR, yR); draw(xP, yP);
      tria(xA, yA,  xR, yR,  xQ, yQ,  n-1);
      tria(xB, yB,  xP, yP,  xR, yR,  n-1);
      tria(xC, yC,  xQ, yQ,  xP, yP,  n-1);
   }
}

main()
{ int n;
  float xA, yA, xB, yB, xC, yC;
  printf("Recursion depth (for example, 7): ");
  scanf("%d", &n);
  initgr();
  xA = 0.0, yA = 0.0;
  xB = x_max; yB = 0.0;
  xC = 0.0; yC = y_max;
  move(xA, yA); draw(xB, yB); draw(xC, yC); draw(xA, yA);
  tria(xA, yA,  xB, yB,  xC, yC,  n);
  endgr();
}
```

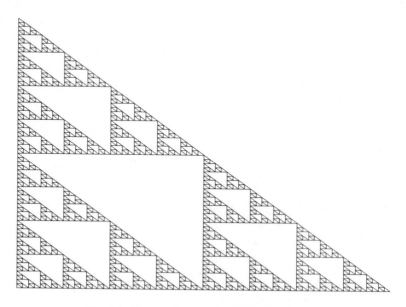

Fig. 4.1. Output of programs TRIANGLES and INTTRIA

Recursive programs are different from non-recursive ones in that it is hardly possible to follow the flow of control in the usual way. As this is often considered to be a problem, it is an advantage for us to write this program without also bothering about pixels, graphics adapters, and a y-axis pointing downward. However, now that program TRIANGLES is ready, we see that its arithmetic is extremely simple, and we also observe that program execution is rather slow if the recursion depth, n, increases. It is therefore a good idea to consider a second version, INTTRIA, which deals only with integers. Its output is identical to that of TRIANGLES, but the program is much faster. Note that INTTRIA combines the fast functions *moveto* and *lineto* of Turbo C with the convenient functions *initgr* and *endgr*, which we have developed ourselves. In this way we have the best of two worlds, so to speak. Due to the use of *initgr*, the maximum pixel coordinates X_max and Y_max are immediately available, so we need not call the functions *getmaxx* and *getmaxy* ourselves.

```c
/* INTTRIA: Fractals based on right triangles.
            Fast version.
*/
#include <stdio.h>
#include "grasptc.h"

void tria(int xA, int yA, int xB, int yB, int xC, int yC, int n)
{ int xP, yP, xQ, yQ, xR, yR;
  if (n > 0)
  { xP = (xB + xC)/2; yP = (yB + yC)/2;
    xQ = (xC + xA)/2; yQ = (yC + yA)/2;
    xR = (xA + xB)/2; yR = (yA + yB)/2;
    moveto(xP, yP); lineto(xQ, yQ);
    lineto(xR, yR); lineto(xP, yP);
    tria(xA, yA,  xR, yR,  xQ, yQ,  n-1);
    tria(xB, yB,  xP, yP,  xR, yR,  n-1);
    tria(xC, yC,  xQ, yQ,  xP, yP,  n-1);
  }
}

main()
{ int n;
  int xA, yA, xB, yB, xC, yC;
  printf("Recursion depth (for example, 7): "); scanf("%d", &n);
  initgr();
  xA = 0, yA = Y__max; xB = X__max; yB = Y__max; xC = 0; yC = 0;
  moveto(xA, yA); lineto(xB, yB); lineto(xC, yC); lineto(xA, yA);
  tria(xA, yA,  xB, yB,  xC, yC,  n);
  endgr();
}
```

4.2 GRAPHICS AND RANDOM NUMBERS

Sometimes we do not want complete symmetry resulting from a straightforward application of recursion. We can then use (pseudo-) random numbers to distort such symmetry to a certain degree. Figure 4.2 was produced in this way. It consists of many occurrences of the capital letter T. Let us call the point at the bottom of the letter T its start point. Beginning with a large T in its normal position, the end points of the horizontal line on the top are in turn start points of new letters T, which are somewhat smaller than the original one. The user of program TTREE is requested to enter two reduction factors (fx and fy), the recursion depth, and a threshold percentage. Each time a new letter T is drawn, a random integer less than 100 is generated. If that integer is less than the given threshold percentage the new letter T has its normal position; otherwise it is drawn upside down. The program uses the well-known formula

$$1 + r + r^2 + \ldots + r^{n-1} = \frac{1 - r^n}{1 - r}$$

to compute the size of the first T, such that the entire result will fit into the screen boundaries.

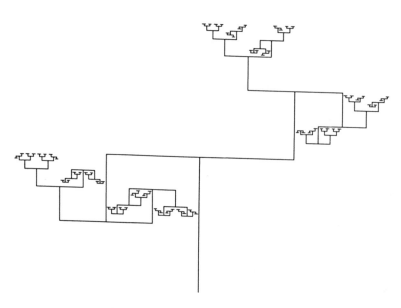

Fig. 4.2. Output of program TTREE

```c
/* TTREE: Letters T, forming a tree.
*/
#include <stdio.h>
#include <stdlib.h>
#include <time.h>
#include "grasptc.h"

float fx, fy, threshold;

void T(float xA, float yA, float a, float b, int n)
{ float xB, yB, xC, yC, xD, yD, a1, b1;
  /* A is lower point of letter T; its (upper) horizontal line
     has end points C (left) and D (right), and midpoint B.
  */
  if (n > 0)
  { xB = xA; yB = yA + a;    /* AB = a      */
    xC = xB - b; yC = yB;    /* CB = BD = b */
    xD = xB + b; yD = yB;
    a1 = fy * a;
    if (a1 < 0) a1 = -a1;
    b1 = fx * b;
    move(xA, yA); draw(xB, yB); draw(xC, yC);
    T(xC, yC, (rand()%100 >= threshold ? -a1 : a1), b1, n-1);
    move(xB, yB); draw(xD, yD);
    T(xD, yD, (rand()%100 >= threshold ? -a1 : a1), b1, n-1);
  }
}


main()
{ float a, b, powerfx, powerfy;
  int n, i;
  long t;
  time(&t); srand((int)t);
  printf("Enter       fx,   fy,   recdepth  upwardpercentage\n");
  printf("(for example, 0.5   0.5     7           70)\n");
  printf("           ");
  scanf("%f %f %d %f", &fx, &fy, &n, &threshold);
  initgr();
  powerfx = fx; powerfy = fy;
  for (i=2; i<=n; i++)
  { powerfx *= fx; powerfy *= fy;
  }
  b = 0.5 * x_max * (1 - fx)/(1 - powerfx);
  a = y_max * (1 - fy)/(1 - powerfy);
  T(x_max/2, y_max/2 - a, a, b, n);
  endgr();
}
```

4.3 RECURSION AND TRANSFORMATIONS

We will now discuss a program in which the following two linear transformations (L and R) are performed:

L:
$$x' = ax + by$$
$$y' = bx - ay$$

R:
$$x' = c(x - x_0) - dy + x_0$$
$$y' = d(x - x_0) + cy$$

To see what transformation L means, we investigate how it behaves with regard to the unit points $(1, 0)$ and $(0, 1)$. By taking $x = 1$ and $y = 0$ we find $x' = a$ and $y' = b$, so the image of $(1, 0)$ is (a, b). Similarly, $(0, 1)$ has $(b, -a)$ as its image. If we take $a = \cos \varphi$ and $b = \sin \varphi$, we see that L is a rotation about O through the angle φ, followed by a reflection about the line that makes an angle φ with the positive x-axis. Together these two operations are equivalent to a reflection about the line that makes an angle $\frac{1}{2}\varphi$ with the positive x-axis. In that case the length of vector (a, b) is equal to 1. In our application that length will be less than 1. We then have a reflection combined with a contraction; the contraction factor is

$$\sqrt{(a^2 + b^2)} < 1$$

Transformation R denotes a rotation about point $(x_0, 0)$, combined with a contraction; here the contraction factor is

$$\sqrt{(c^2 + d^2)} < 1$$

The most interesting thing, however, is not these transformations themselves but the way we will use them. Let us denote our start point, $(1, 0)$ by **u**. We now apply L to **u**, which gives a new point, say L**u**. We also apply R to **u**, which gives the new point R**u**. Then we again (independently) apply L and R to each of these new points, which gives the four new points LL**u**, RL**u**, LR**u**, RR**u**. To each of these four new points we apply both L and R again, which gives eight new points, and so on. It will be clear that the whole process is similar to drawing a binary tree, as we did in Section 4.2.

You may have wondered if our start point **u** = $(1, 0)$ can be of any use, given our coordinate system and the screen boundaries. Recall that in Section 4.2 we could compute the size of the first letter T so that the final result fitted into the screen boundaries. If such an analytic approach is too complicated or even impossible, there is always another method available, which we will use here. We simply compute all points twice; the first time, instead of plotting them, we merely use them to find the least and the greatest values of all x- and y-coordinates that the new points have, based on the start point $\mathbf{u} = (1, 0)$. We then compare the ranges thus found with those available in our coordinate system. Dividing the latter ranges by the former gives us the scaling factors fx and fy. We use the smaller of these, and reduce it somewhat to have some blank margins. This provides us with the scaling factor f that we will use. Besides the computed ranges, we are also interested in the center of the computed coordinates, so that we can make it coincide with the center of our screen.

So much for our solution of the scaling problem. It may be observed that instead of computing everything twice, we can store the points, either in memory or on disk, and use them later. This approach is attractive if the computations involved are very time-consuming. In program TRANSFOR all points are computed twice. With a 8088 processor, computation is not a lengthy process as long as the recursion depth is not greater than 10, but it takes several hours if it is 18, as I experienced when producing Fig. 4.3. It is always annoying if the computer is doing a lot of computing without displaying anything on the screen. Program TRANSFOR therefore displays a counter which ranges from 1 to 32 when, in the text mode, it is computing the boundaries. We simply increase this counter by 1 each time we are at recursion depth 5. Then we switch to the graphics mode, and now 32 dots, lying 8 pixels apart, are successively displayed on a horizontal line at the top of the screen; as soon as the last dot is displayed, all these dots are removed, which indicates that the final result is on the screen. Especially with high values of the recursion depth this is very useful, because otherwise it may not be clear whether or not the image on the screen has been completed, and, if not, how much time will still be needed.

You can use this program to generate all kinds of attractive point patterns, although most sets of input data give results that are not worthwhile. After many experiments I used the input data

recursion depth = 18, a = 0.7, b = 0.3, c = 0.5, d = 0.3, $x0$ = 1.0.

to obtain Fig. 4.3. Figures with a recurring similarity, as we have here, are called *fractals*. With increasing recursion depth, enlarged details of a fractal are similar to the whole.

```
/* TRANSFOR: Recursion and transformations.
*/

#include <stdio.h>
#include "grasptc.h"

float xreal(float x);
float yreal(float y);
```

```
void transf(float x, float y, int n, int prescan);
float fx, fy, f, xC, yC, xmin0=100, xmax0=-100, ymin0=100,
      ymax0=-100, xC0, yC0, a, b, c, d, x0, x, y;
int count=0, recdepth, level_5;

main()
{ int i;
  printf("Recursion depth (e.g. 12): ");
  scanf("%d", &recdepth); level_5 = recdepth - 5;
  printf("Enter a, b, c, d, x0 (e.g.  .7  .3  .5  .3  1):\n");
  scanf("%f %f %f %f %f", &a, &b, &c, &d, &x0);
  printf("Please wait; counter has final value 32:\n");
  transf(1.0, 0.0, recdepth, 1);
  initgr();
  fx = x_max/(xmax0 - xmin0);
  fy = y_max/(ymax0 - ymin0);
  f = (fx < fy ? fx : fy) * 0.8;
  xC0 = (xmin0 + xmax0)/2; yC0 = (ymin0 + ymax0)/2;
  xC = x_max/2; yC - y_max/2;
  count = 0;
  transf(1.0, 0.0, recdepth, 0);
  for (i=1; i<=32; i++) putpixel(8*i, 0, backgrcolor);
  endgr();
}


void transf(float x, float y, int n, int prescan)
{ float x1, y1;
  if (n > 0)
  { if (prescan)
    { if (n == level_5) printf("%d ", ++count);
      if (x < xmin0) xmin0 = x;
      if (x > xmax0) xmax0 = x;
      if (y < ymin0) ymin0 = y;
      if (y > ymax0) ymax0 = y;
    } else
    { if (n == level_5) putpixel(count+=8, 0, foregrcolor);
      putpixel(IX(xreal(x)), IY(yreal(y)), foregrcolor);
    }
    x1 = a * x + b * y;
    y1 = b * x - a * y;
      /* Reflection and contraction; (0, 0) is fixed point */
    transf(x1, y1, n-1, prescan);
    x1 = c * (x-x0) - d * y + x0;
    y1 = d * (x-x0) + c * y;
      /* Rotation and contraction; (x0, 0) is fixed point  */
    transf(x1, y1, n-1, prescan);
  }
}
```

```
float xreal(float x)
{ return xC + f * (x - xC0);
}

float yreal(float y)
{ return yC + f * (y - yC0);
}
```

Fig. 4.3. Sample result of program TRANSFOR

4.4 HILBERT CURVES

Recursion can also be used to obtain line patterns called *Hilbert curves*. A Hilbert curve is based on the letter U, drawn as three sides of a square, as shown (upside down) on the left in Fig. 4.4. There are Hilbert curves of order 1, 2, ..., denoted by H_1, H_2, ... In the middle of Fig. 4.4, we see H_2, in which some line segments, the so-called *links*, are drawn as bold lines. Actually, these line segments should have the same thickness as the others; they are bold here only to explain how H_2 can be derived from H_1 (shown on the left). We see that H_2 can be regarded as a large letter U with four portions of it replaced with smaller letters U. The latter are connected by three links. Each side of a small U has the same length as a link; they are three times as small as the sides of the square in which H_2 fits. We now apply this process to each of the four letters U of H_2, so we replace each U in H_2 with a smaller H_2; we also reduce the links so that their lengths become equal to the elementary line segments that occur in the three small H_2 figures. In this way, we obtain H_3, shown in Fig. 4.4 on the right. All elementary line segments are now seven times as small as the square in which H_3 fits. We see that reduction factors for these elementary line segment in H_1, H_2, H_3, ... are 1, 3, 7, ..., so, in general, the reduction factor for H_n is $2^n - 1$.

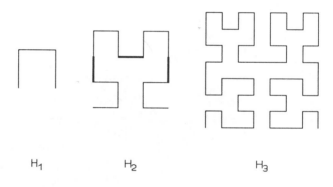

H_1 H_2 H_3

Fig. 4.4. Hilbert curves of order 1, 2, and 3

Note that the links in H_2 are drawn in the same directions as the three line segments of H_1. If we like, we can regard the latter line segments as links, connecting four points, which we may regard as Hilbert curves of order 0.

In our program for Hilbert curves we will use a recursive function *Hilbert*, with the following arguments:

- The coordinates of the points A, B, and C (see Fig. 4.5).

- The horizontal and vertical components of the two directed links: one lying on AB and the other on AC. They are given as vectors, that is, as pairs (dx, dy), where dx and dy can be positive, zero, or negative, depending on the relative positions of A, B, and C. These two vectors are called **dAB** and **dAC** in the program.

- The recursion depth, n. For $n = 0$ the function has to do nothing at all.

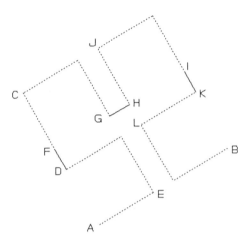

Fig. 4.5. Construction of points in a Hilbert curve

We imagine Fig. 4.5 to be a variation of the letter U (rotated clockwise through 150°), whose position is fully determined by the three given points A, B, and C. We regard point A as the start point and point B as the end point. The main reason point C is given is to indicate whether the curve to be drawn should lie on the left or on the right side of the directed line AB. The two given link vectors, **dAB** and **dAC**, can be seen as links in Fig. 4.5 at three places, namely as DF, GH, and IK. The three given points A, B, C and the two given vectors **dAB** and **dAC** enable us to find the positions of the points D, E, F, G, H, I, J, K in Fig. 4.5. (We will not require CAB to be a right angle, nor need AB be as long as AC, so instead of forming a square, each letter U may have the shape of any parallelogram.) In general, the dotted lines in Fig. 4.5 will not actually be drawn. Instead, we perform a recursive call to our function *Hilbert* for each of the four dashed letters U of Fig. 4.5. We also call our function *draw* to draw the three links DF, GH, and IK.

Fig. 4.6. Output of program HILBERT

```
/* HILBERT: Hilbert curves of any order.
*/
#include "grasptc.h"

typedef struct {float x, y;} vec;
int recdepth, steps;

void Hilbert(vec A, vec B, vec C, vec dAB, vec dAC, int n)
{ vec D, E, F, G, H, I, J, K, L;
  if (n > 0)
  { D.x = (A.x + C.x - dAC.x)/2;
    D.y = (A.y + C.y - dAC.y)/2;
    E.x = (A.x + B.x - dAB.x)/2;
    E.y = (A.y + B.y - dAB.y)/2;
    F.x = D.x + dAC.x; F.y = D.y + dAC.y;
    G.x = F.x + E.x - A.x; G.y = F.y + E.y - A.y;
    H.x = G.x + dAB.x; H.y = G.y + dAB.y;
    I.x = F.x + B.x - A.x; I.y = F.y + B.y - A.y;
    J.x = C.x + H.x - F.x; J.y = C.y + H.y - F.y;
    K.x = I.x - dAC.x; K.y = I.y - dAC.y;
    L.x = H.x - dAC.x; L.y = H.y - dAC.y;
    Hilbert(A, D, E, dAC, dAB, n-1);
```

```
    draw(F.x, F.y);          /* Link DF */
    Hilbert(F, G, C, dAB, dAC, n-1);
    draw(H.x, H.y);          /* Link GH */
    Hilbert(H, I, J, dAB, dAC, n-1);
    draw(K.x, K.y);          /* Link IK */
    dAB.x = -dAB.x; dAB.y = -dAB.y;
    dAC.x = -dAC.x; dAC.y = -dAC.y;
    /*  These changes in dAB and dAC apply
        only to local copies
    */
    Hilbert(K, B, L, dAC, dAB, n-1);
  }
}

void square(float xA, float yA, float xB, float yB, float xC, float yC)
{ vec A, B, C, dAB, dAC;
  A.x = xA; A.y = yA;
  B.x = xB; B.y = yB;
  C.x = xC; C.y = yC;
  dAB.x = (xB - xA)/steps;
  dAB.y = (yB - yA)/steps;
  dAC.x = (xC - xA)/steps;
  dAC.y = (yC - yA)/steps;
  move(xA, yA);
  Hilbert(A, B, C, dAB, dAC, recdepth);
}

main()
{ float xCenter, yCenter, h, xP, yP, xQ, yQ, xR, yR;
  printf("Enter the recursion depth: ");
  scanf("%d", &recdepth);
  steps = (1 << recdepth) - 1;
  /* steps = power(2, recdepth) - 1
  */
  initgr();
  xCenter = x_max/2;
  yCenter = y_max/2;
  h = y_max/40;
  xP = xR = xCenter - 3 * h;
  xQ = xCenter + 3 * h;
  yP = yQ = yCenter - 4 * h;
  yR = yCenter + 4 * h;
  square(xQ, yQ, xR, yR, xQ+8*h, yQ+6*h); /* Right square */
  square(xR, yR, xP, yP, xR-8*h, yR);     /* Left square  */
  square(xP, yP, xQ, yQ, xP, yP-6*h);     /* Lower square */
  endgr();
}
```

4.5 DRAGON CURVES

Curves with recurring patterns need not always be generated by means of recursive functions. We consider a curve that we can regard as being obtained by repeatedly folding a long strip of paper in a systematic way. If we have folded it three times, and unfold it a little so that all angles become equal to 90°, we obtain Fig. 4.7. If you find this difficult to understand, just imagine the angle at point M in the middle to become increasingly smaller; when it is zero, we again let the angle in the middle become smaller, and so on.

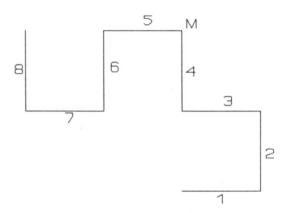

Fig. 4.7. Dragon curve of eight elements

If we follow the curve, starting at line segment 1, then at each corner we have to turn 90° either right or left. The problem to be solved is how to turn (left or right) at the end of each line segment i (i = 1, 2, ...). Let us use code 1 for turning left and 3 for turning right, and denote the code for line segment i by $T(i)$. (Then we can say that at the end of line segment i we have to turn $T(i) \times$ 90° to the left, for rotating clockwise through 90° is equivalent to turning 270° counterclockwise.) In Fig. 4.7 we can see that

$$T(1) = 1, \, T(2) = 1, \, T(3) = 3, \, T(4) = 1, \, T(5) = 1, \, T(6) = 3, \, T(7) = 3$$

We can investigate a similar curve of 16 line segments in the same way, and so on. It then appears that function T can be defined as follows for any natural number i, using the operators / and % for the quotient and the remainder of integer division:

$T(i) = T(i \: / \: 2)$ if i is even;
$T(i) = i \: \% \: 4$ if i is odd.

Although the former formula is recursive, the curves in question can easily be generated by a non-recursive program. Incidentally, curves of this type are called *dragon curves*, which explains the name of program DRAGON. As in Section 4.3, we compute the curve twice, so that we can make the figure fit into the screen boundaries. Here this method is very efficient because we can use integers instead of floating-point variables. This is possible because all line segments have the same length, and internally we can use any unit of length. After all, the real dimensions of the line segments are computed only just before we draw them.

A remarkable characteristic of dragon curves is that they do not intersect themselves. We can demonstrate this very clearly by rounding all corners, or rather by replacing them with small line segments so that everywhere we have angles of 135° instead of 90°. The only input data for program DRAGON is the number of (horizontal and vertical) line segments to be drawn. Although the program accepts any number, this number should be a power of 2 if a proper dragon curve is desired. For example, in Fig. 4.8 there are 256 line segments; this number is small enough to let you clearly see the rounded corners.

```
/* DRAGON: Dragon curve
*/
#include <stdio.h>
#include "grasptc.h"
int x=0, y=0, dx=4, dy=0, n, xmin=10, xmax=-10,
    ymin=10, ymax=-10, ixC, iyC;
float fx, fy, f, xC, yC;

float xreal(int x);
float yreal(int y);
void curve(int prescan);
void step(int r, int prescan);

main()
{ printf("How many line segments? (e.g. 256): ");
  scanf("%d", &n);
  curve(1);
  initgr();
  fx = x_max/(xmax - xmin); fy = y_max/(ymax - ymin);
  f = (fx < fy ? fx : fy) * 0.7;
  ixC = (xmin + xmax)/2;
  iyC = (ymin + ymax)/2;
  xC = x_max/2;
  yC = y_max/2;
  x = y = 0; dx=4; dy=0;
```

```
    move(xreal(x+dx/4), yreal(y));
    curve(0);
    endgr();
}

void curve(int prescan)
{ int i, j, r;
  for (i=1; i<=n; i++)
  { j=i;
    while ((j & 1) == 0) j >>= 1;
    r = j & 3;
    step(r, prescan);
  }
}

void step(int r, int prescan)
{ int t, dx1, dy1;
  if (prescan)
  { x += dx; y += dy;
    if (x < xmin) xmin = x;
    if (x > xmax) xmax = x;
    if (y < ymin) ymin = y;
    if (y > ymax) ymax = y;
  } else
  { dx1 = dx/4; dy1 = dy/4;
    draw(xreal(x + dx1), yreal(y + dy1));
    x += dx; y += dy;
    draw(xreal(x - dx1), yreal(y - dy1));
  }
  if (r == 1) {t = dx; dx = -dy; dy = t;} else
  /* r == 3 */ {t = dx; dx = dy; dy = -t;}

}


float xreal(int x)
{ return xC + f * (x - ixC);
}

float yreal(int y)
{ return yC + f * (y - iyC);
}
```

Fig. 4.8. Dragon curve with rounded corners

4.6 CIRCLES AND SQUARES

Circles

Many attractive patterns can be produced by functions that perform two tasks: first, they draw a figure, for example a circle, with a center and size given as arguments, and second, they call themselves recursively to draw the same figure, but smaller than the original one, several times. Figure 4.9 has been obtained in this way.

It is always annoying if users have to worry about the screen boundaries. This will not be the case for program CIRCLES, which can produce Fig. 4.9 and many similar patterns. Program CIRCLES does not require any input data about the absolute size of the figure. Instead, we have to enter the data listed below. The corresponding program-variable names and the particular values for Fig. 4.9 are given in parentheses.

1 The recursion depth which indicates here how many different circles there are ($n = 4$).
2 The reduction factor to compute the radius of each satellite circle from that of its base circle ($f = 0.3$).
3 The factor by which the radius of a circle is to be multiplied to obtain the radius of the (circular) 'orbit' of its satellites ($c = 2.0$).

4 The number of circles in each orbit ($nsatellite$ = 8).
5 A code (1 or 0) to indicate whether or not an HP-GL file is desired. If so, the name of this file will be CIRCLES.HPG (hpg = 1).

The circles in Fig. 4.9 have four different sizes. Let us say that the largest circle has radius r. Then the other circles have radii fr, f^2r, f^3r. We will write $R = cr$ for the radius of the largest orbit: the centers of the largest and the second largest circles lie a distance R apart. Then fR and f^2R are the radii of the other orbits. This means that the distance between the centers of the (large) innermost and a (small) outermost circle is equal to

$$R + fR + f^2R$$

As we want to relate this to the available space on the screen to compute R, we have to bear in mind that the smallest circle, although possibly very small indeed, also takes up some space, so we have to add its radius to the above sum. A simple and safe way of dealing with this problem is to add another term (which means that we allocate space for another orbit, as if n were 1 higher than it is).

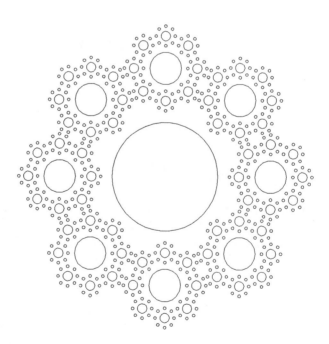

Fig. 4.9. Output of program CIRCLES

So if $n = 4$, we will use the sum

$$R + fR + f^2R + f^3R$$

In general this distance is equal to

$$\begin{aligned} s &= R + fR + f^2R + \ldots + f^{n-1}R \\ &= R(1 + f + f^2 + \ldots + f^{n-1}) \\ &= R(1 - f^n)/(1 - f) \end{aligned}$$

(If you are not familiar with the sum of a finite geometric series, you can verify the last equality simply by checking that the product $(1 - f)(1 + f + f^2 + \ldots + f^{n-1})$ gives $1 - f^n$.) In program CIRCLES, we compute the power f^n in the variable p. As y_max is less than x_max, it is important that the above sum s should not be larger than $y\_max/2$. It follows that the radii R and r of the largest orbit and the largest circle, respectively, can be computed as follows:

```
R = 0.5 * y_max * (1 - f)/(1 - p);
r = R/c;
```

The rest of program CIRCLES is not difficult to understand, so we will not discuss it in detail.

```
/* CIRCLES: This program uses a recursive function to draw circles.
*/
#include <stdio.h>
#include <stdlib.h>
#include <math.h>
#include "grasptc.h"
float f;
int nsatellite, hpg;
float ccos[100], csin[100];

void scircle(float x, float y, float r) /* Used only if hpg = 1 */
{ int n=(int)(30 * r + 8), i;
  float theta=2*PI/n;
  move(x+r, y);
  for (i=1; i<=n; i++) draw(x+r*cos(i*theta), y+r*sin(i*theta));
}

void circles(float x, float y, float r, int n)
{ int i, n1=n-1;
  float fr=f*r;
  if (n-- > 0)
  { if (hpg == 1) scircle(x, y, r); else circle_uc(x, y, r);
    for (i=0; i<nsatellite; i++)
    circles(x+r*ccos[i], y+r*csin[i], fr, n1);
```

```
    }
  }

  main()
  { int n, i;
    float p=1, r, R, c, theta;
    printf("Recursion depth (e.g. 4): "); scanf("%d", &n);
    printf("Reduction factor (e.g. 0.3): "); scanf("%f", &f);
    printf("For a circle with radius r, the orbit of its satellites\n");
    printf("will be a circle with radius cr.\n");
    printf("Enter c (e.g. 2.0): "); scanf("%f", &c);
    for (i=0; i<n; i++) p *= f;
    printf("Number of satellite circles (for example: 8): ");
    scanf("%d", &nsatellite);
    printf("Type 1 if you want an HP-GL file, and 0 otherwise: ");
    scanf("%d", &hpg);
    if (hpg == 1) fplot = fopen("circles.hpg", "w");
    if (nsatellite > 100) exit(1);
    theta = 2 * PI/nsatellite;
    for (i=0; i<nsatellite; i++)
    { ccos[i] = c * cos(i * theta);
      csin[i] = c * sin(i * theta);
    }
    initgr();
    R = 0.5 * y_max * (1-f)/(1-p); r = R/c;
    circles(x_max/2, y_max/2, r, n);
    endgr();
  }
```

Squares

We can use squares (or other figures) in the same way as we have just been
using circles. Program SQUARES, listed below, is similar to the program
CIRCLES we have been discussing, but demonstrates some new aspects as well.
First, we can choose between open and filled squares. If they are open, the whole
figure consists only of line segments. In that case, the program also generates the
file SQUARES.HPG, containing HP-GL code. If desired, the program can also
omit squares that lie between each satellite square and its base square. Figure
4.10 shows filled squares, with normally four satellites per square, whereas in Fig.
4.11 there are only three. In Fig. 4.10 the satellites of each square were drawn
before that square itself, so that satellites were partly overwritten by their base
squares. If you want it the other way round, you can simply move the call to
square1 four lines higher, that is, just after the open brace, in the function
squares.

Fig. 4.10. Filled squares

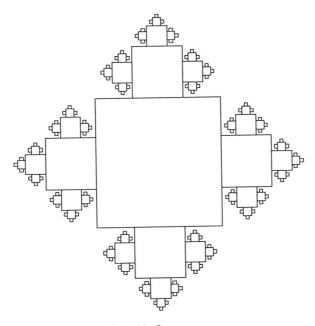

Fig. 4.11. Open squares

Figure 4.11 is a special case: by choosing $f = 0.4$ and $c = 1.4$, so that we have

$$c = 1 + f$$

there is no gap between each satellite square and its base; nor do they overlap.

```
/* SQUARES: This program uses a recursive function to
            draw squares.
*/
#define EAST 1
#define NORTH 2
#define WEST 3
#define SOUTH 4
#include <stdio.h>
#include <stdlib.h>
#include <math.h>
#include "grasptc.h"
float f, c;
int filling, all4;

void square1(float x, float y, float r)
{ float xA, yA, xB, yB, xC, yC, xD, yD;
  int points[10];
  xA = x-r; yA = y-r;
  xB = x+r; yB = y-r;
  xC = x+r; yC = y+r;
  xD = x-r; yD = y+r;
  if (filling)
  { points[0] = IX(xA); points[1] = IY(yA);
    points[2] = IX(xB); points[3] = IY(yB);
    points[4] = IX(xC); points[5] = IY(yC);
    points[6] = IX(xD); points[7] = IY(yD);
    points[8] = points[0]; points[9] = points[1];
    fillpoly(5, points);
  } else
  { move(xA, yA); draw(xB, yB);
    draw(xC, yC); draw(xD, yD); draw(xA, yA);
    /* Here we use 'move' and 'draw' rather than 'drawpoly',
       to produce the output file SQUARES.HPG.
    */
  }
}

void squares(float x, float y, float r, int n, int dir)
{ int n1=n-1;
  float fr=f*r, cr=c*r;
  if (n > 0)
```

```
{ if (dir != WEST || all4) squares(x+cr, y, fr, n1, EAST);
  if (dir != SOUTH || all4) squares(x, y+cr, fr, n1, NORTH);
  if (dir != EAST || all4) squares(x-cr, y, fr, n1, WEST);
  if (dir != NORTH || all4) squares(x, y-cr, fr, n1, SOUTH);
  square1(x, y, r);
 }
}

main()
{ int n, i, m;
  float p=1, r, R;
  printf("Recursion depth (for example: 5): ");
  scanf("%d", &n);
  printf("Reduction factor (for example: 0.5): ");
  scanf("%f", &f);
  printf("\nFor a square with sides at a distance r from its center P\n");
  printf("its satellites squares will have centers at a distance cr\n");
  printf("from point P.\n");
  printf("Enter c (for example: 2.0): ");
  scanf("%f", &c);
  for (i=0; i<n; i++) p *= f;
  printf("Type 1 if the squares are to be filled, and 0 otherwise: ");
  scanf("%d", &filling);
  if (!filling) fplot = fopen("squares.hpg", "w");
  do
  { printf("Do you want 3 or 4 satellites per square? ");
    scanf("%d", &m);
  } while (m < 3 || m > 4);
  all4 = (m == 4);
  initgr();
  setfillstyle(CLOSE_DOT_FILL, foregrcolor);
  R = y_max/2.2 * (1-f)/(1-p); r = R/c;
  squares(x_max/2, y_max/2, r, n, 0);
  endgr();
 }
```

It is also possible to apply the principle of base and satellite figures to three dimensions. We then obtain a three-dimensional object, say, a sphere, with smaller spheres as satellites. These satellites again have satellites, and so on. This is similar to the earth, which is a satellite of the sun but has in turn the moon as its satellite. Figure 4.12 shows a situation where satellites 'on the inner side' have been omitted, as we did with the squares in Fig. 4.11.

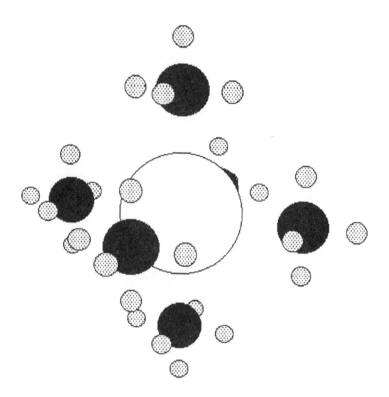

Fig. 4.12. Perspective view of spheres

Figure 4.12 was produced by program SPHERES. This performs a coordinate transformation, to switch from the original 'world-coordinate system' (x, y, z) to an 'eye-coordinate system' (x_e, y_e, z_e) with the origin in the viewpoint and the z-axis pointing to the object. You can find a discussion of this in *Programming Principles in Computer Graphics*, and, more briefly, in *Interactive 3D Computer Graphics*. However, program SPHERES does not use the hidden-line algorithm of those books; it is based on a fundamentally different way of displaying only visible spheres and visible portions of them. First, we know that we always see a sphere as a circle, regardless of the viewpoint. We therefore compute only the centers, the radii of the circles that will appear on the screen, along with the z_e coordinates of the sphere centers. Instead of drawing them, we store them in an array. We sort this array, using the stored z_e value as a key. Then we draw all spheres, in decreasing order of their z_e values. Each sphere is drawn as a circle, filled with the background color. In this way the spheres that are close to the eye are drawn last and if their place on the screen is already used by another sphere, then that one is overwritten. The principle used is known as the *painter's algorithm*, because it is similar to the way paintings can be made.

```c
/* SPHERES: Spheres in perspective.
*/
#include <stdlib.h>
#include <math.h>
#include "grasptc.h"

#define TABLELENGTH 3000
#define EAST 1
#define WEST 2
#define NORTH 3
#define SOUTH 4
#define UP 5
#define DOWN 6

int m;
float Xmin=1000, Xmax=-1000, Ymin=1000, Ymax=-1000, C, F;
struct sph {float X, Y, ze, R; int rdepth;} table[TABLELENGTH];

float v11, v12, v13, v21, v22, v23, v32, v33, v43,
      f, XC, YC, xC, yC;

void coeff(float rho, float theta, float phi)
{ float costh, sinth, cosph, sinph;
  costh=cos(theta); sinth=sin(theta);
  cosph=cos(phi); sinph=sin(phi);
  v11=-sinth; v12=-cosph*costh; v13=-sinph*costh;
  v21=costh;  v22=-cosph*sinth; v23=-sinph*sinth;
              v32=sinph;        v33=-cosph;
                                v43=rho;
}

void perspective(float x, float y, float z,
                 float *pX, float *pY, float *pze)
{ float xe, ye, ze;

  /* Eye coordinates */
  xe = v11*x + v21*y;
  ye = v12*x + v22*y + v32*z;
  ze = v13*x + v23*y + v33*z + v43;

  /* Screen coordinates */
  *pX = xe/ze;
  *pY = ye/ze;
  *pze = ze;
}
```

```
void sphere1(float x, float y, float z, float r, int n)
{ float X, Y, Xtop, Ytop, R, ze, zetop;
  perspective(x, y, z, &X, &Y, &ze);
  if (X < Xmin) Xmin = X;
  if (X > Xmax) Xmax = X;
  if (Y < Ymin) Ymin = Y;
  if (Y > Ymax) Ymax = Y;
  perspective(x, y, z+r, &Xtop, &Ytop, &zetop);
  R = Ytop - Y;
  table[m].X = X; table[m].Y = Y; table[m].ze = ze; table[m].R = R;
  table[m].rdepth = n;
  if (++m == TABLELENGTH)
  { printf("Too many spheres"); exit(1);
  }
  if (m % 20 == 0) printf("m = %d\n", m);
}

void spheres(float x, float y, float z, float r, float n, float dir)
{ int n1=n-1;
  float fr=F*r, cr=C*r;
  if (n > 0)
  { sphere1(x, y, z, r, n);
    if (dir != WEST) spheres(x+cr, y, z, fr, n1, EAST);
    if (dir != EAST) spheres(x-cr, y, z, fr, n1, WEST);
    if (dir != SOUTH) spheres(x, y+cr, z, fr, n1, NORTH);
    if (dir != NORTH) spheres(x, y-cr, z, fr, n1, SOUTH);
    if (dir != DOWN) spheres(x, y, z+cr, fr, n1, UP);
    if (dir != UP) spheres(x, y, z-cr, fr, n1, DOWN);
  }
}


float xreal(float X)
{ return xC + f*(X - XC);
}


float yreal(float Y)
{ return yC + f*(Y - YC);
}


void quicksort(int l, int r)
/* This sorting algorithm is discussed in many books,
   such as, for example, PROGRAMS AND DATA STRUCTURES IN C.
*/
{ int i=l, j=r;
  float pivot=table[(l+r)/2].ze;
  struct sph w;
  do
  { while (table[i].ze < pivot) i++;
```

```
    while (table[j].ze > pivot) j--;
    if (i > j) break;
    w = table[i]; table[i] = table[j]; table[j] = w;
  } while (++i <= --j);
  if (l < j) quicksort(l, j);
  if (i < r) quicksort(i, r);
}


void main(void)
{ float rho, theta, phi, fx, fy, xx, yy, rr;
  int recdepth, i, X, Y, RX, RY, code, fill;
  printf("Enter the reduction factors c and f (e.g. 2  0.4): ");
  scanf("%f %f", &C, &F);
  printf("Viewing distance (e.g. 12): "); scanf("%f", &rho);
  printf("Give two angles, in degrees.\n");
  printf("Theta, measured horizontally from the x-axis (e.g. 20): ");
  scanf("%f", &theta); theta *= PI/180;
  printf("Phi, measured vertically from the z-axis (e.g. 75): ");
  scanf("%f", &phi); phi *= PI/180;
  printf("Recursion depth (e.g. 3): "); scanf("%d", &recdepth);
  coeff(rho, theta, phi);
  spheres(0.0, 0.0, 0.0, 1.0, recdepth, 0);
  quicksort(0, m-1);
  initgr();
  xC = x_max/2;
  yC = y_max/2;
  XC = (Xmin+Xmax)/2;
  YC = (Ymin+Ymax)/2;
  fx = x_max/(Xmax-Xmin);
  fy = y_max/(Ymax-Ymin);
  f = 0.9 * (fx < fy ? fx : fy);
  for (i=m-1; i>=0; i--)
  { xx = xreal(table[i].X); X = IX(xx);
    yy = yreal(table[i].Y); Y = IY(yy);
    rr = f * table[i].R;
    RX = XPIX(rr); RY = YPIX(rr);
    code = table[i].rdepth % 3;
    fill = (code == 2 ? SOLID_FILL :
            code == 1 ? CLOSE_DOT_FILL : EMPTY_FILL);
    setfillstyle(fill, foregrcolor);
    fillellipse(X, Y, RX, RY);
  }
  endgr();
}
```

4.7 FRACTALS

In Fig. 4.11 all squares were connected, so it is possible to draw only the outside edge (the circumference) of the whole figure. This is shown by Fig. 4.13, produced by program SQFRACT. With increasing recursion depth, we obtain a closed region, the boundary of which becomes very large compared with its area. Closed curves like these are called *fractal curves* or *fractals*. A fractal is like an island with a coastline that looks smooth from a distance but becomes increasingly irregular as we approach it.

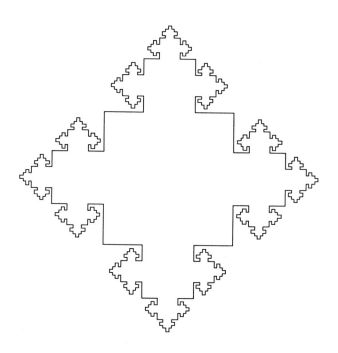

Fig. 4.13. Outer edges of squares, drawn as one curve

```
/* SQFRACT: This program draws a fractal based on squares.
*/
#include <stdio.h>
#include <stdlib.h>
#include <math.h>
#include "grasptc.h"
float f, fact;
```

```
void side(float xA, float yA, float xB, float yB,
          int n)
{ float xP, yP, xQ, yQ, xR, yR, xS, yS, fdx, fdy;
  /* Current pen position is (xA, yA) */
  if (n == 0) draw(xB, yB); else
  { fdx = fact * (xB-xA); fdy = fact * (yB-yA);
    xP = xA + fdx; yP = yA + fdy;
    xS = xB - fdx; yS = yB - fdy;
    xQ = xP + (yS - yP); yQ = yP - (xS - xP);
    xR = xQ + (xS - xP); yR = yQ + (yS - yP);
    draw(xP, yP);
    side(xP, yP, xQ, yQ, n-1);
    side(xQ, yQ, xR, yR, n-1);
    side(xR, yR, xS, yS, n-1);
    draw(xB, yB);
  }
}

main()
{ int n, i;
  float p=1, r, R, xC, yC;
  printf("Recursion depth (for example: 5): ");
  scanf("%d", &n);
  printf("Reduction factor (for example: 0.4): ");
  scanf("%f", &f);
  for (i=0; i<n; i++) p *= f;
  fact = 0.5*(1-f);
  initgr();
  R = y_max/2.2 * (1-f)/(1-p); r = R/(1+f);
  xC = x_max/2; yC = y_max/2;
  move(xC-r, yC-r);
  side(xC-r, yC-r, xC+r, yC-r, n);
  side(xC+r, yC-r, xC+r, yC+r, n);
  side(xC+r, yC+r, xC-r, yC+r, n);
  side(xC-r, yC+r, xC-r, yC-r, n);
  endgr();
}
```

The first four arguments of function *side* are the coordinates of both end points
A and B of a line segment. Only if the fifth argument, n, is equal to 0 will this
line segment be drawn. Otherwise, two new points, P and S, are constructed on
it. These are the end points of a side of a smaller square (with PS = f . AB), as
shown in Fig. 4.14. Here we also see that we can find the coordinates of point Q
as follows:

$$x_Q = x_P + (y_S - y_P)$$
$$y_Q = y_P - (x_S - x_P)$$

(Recall that we have discussed a similar construction of a new point in more detail when dealing with Hilbert curves in Section 4.4.) Finally, we can find point R easily, since it relates to Q as S relates to P. Then we simply draw AP, apply the function recursively to the sides PQ, QR, RS of the smaller square, and conclude by drawing SB.

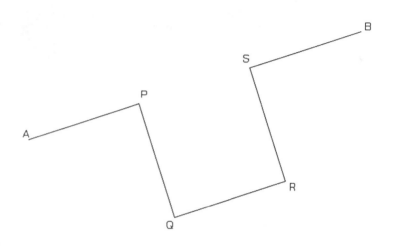

Fig. 4.14. Construction of P, Q, R, S

Instead of drawing AP and SB, we could also apply *side* recursively to these two line segments. Although it may not give a satisfactory result in this particular case, the idea is very useful. It leads to a class of very interesting new curves, which consist of straight line segments that, unlike Fig. 4.13, have (about) the same lengths. (Recall that this is also the case with Hilbert curves, as we have discussed in Section 3.3.)

We shall consider a very general program to generate such curves. First, the base figure can be either a horizontal line segment or any regular polygon. Second, instead of computing the positions of the new points P, Q, R, S (the *model points*) relative to A and B, as in Fig. 4.14, the user has to supply any number of such points (not necessarily four) as input data. To this end we introduce a local coordinate system, with A in (0, 0) and B in (1, 0). The model points are then to be expressed in these local coordinates. Consider, for example, Fig. 4.15, where we have three new points, with coordinates

x	y
0.45	0
0.50	0.45
0.55	0

Remember that the two end point A(0, 0) and B(1, 0) are implicitly added to the model points that we enter, so the total number of model points is always two higher than those we specify.

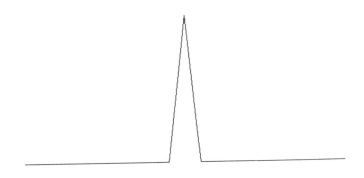

Fig. 4.15. Basic pattern with three new points

If the pattern of the whole is applied to its four parts we obtain Fig. 4.16, and so on. As we can ask for a regular polygon, for example, with four sides, it will be clear that program FRCURVE, in which this has been implemented, can also produce Fig. 4.17.

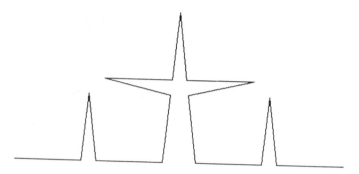

Fig. 4.16. Recursive application of the basic pattern

If the pattern of the whole is applied to its three parts, we obtain Fig. 4.16, and so on. As we can ask for a regular polygon, for example, with four sides, it will be clear that program FRCURVE, in which this has been implemented, can also produce Fig. 4.17.

Fig. 4.17. The same pattern applied to the sides of a square

```c
/* FRCURVE: This program replaces either one horizontal line or
            each side of a regular polygon with a fractal curve
            of any given shape.
*/
#include <stdio.h>
#include <stdlib.h>
#include <math.h>
#include "grasptc.h"
int nmodel;
float xx[30], yy[30];

void side(float xA, float yA, float xB, float yB,
          int n)
{ int i;
  float x, y, x1, y1, dx=xB-xA, dy=yB-yA;
  if (n == 0)
  { move(xA, yA); draw(xB, yB);
  } else
  { x1 = xA; y1 = yA;
    for (i=1; i<=nmodel; i++)
    { x = x1; y = y1;
      x1 = xA + dx * xx[i] - dy * yy[i];
      y1 = yA + dy * xx[i] + dx * yy[i];
      side(x, y, x1, y1, n-1);
    }
  }
}


main()
{ int n, k, i;
  float pi, theta, r, x, y, x1, y1, xC, yC,
        sizefactor, xmargin, phi;
  printf("Enter 1 if you want the base to be a horizontal line.\n");
  printf("For a regular polygon with k sides as base, enter k\n");
  printf("(for example: 4): ");
  scanf("%d", &k);
  printf("\nRecursion depth (for example: 4): ");
  scanf("%d", &n);
  printf("\nHow many model points between (0, 0) and (1, 0)\n");
  printf("(for example: 3): ");
  scanf("%d", &nmodel);
  nmodel++;
  /* Now nmodel is the number of line segments
     between (0, 0) and (1, 0).
  */
  printf("Enter the pairs (x, y) for your model "   "points,\n");
  printf("excluding (0, 0) and 1, 0),\n");
  printf("(for example:\n.45  0\n.5  .45\n.55  0):\n\n");
```

```
for (i=1; i<nmodel; i++) scanf("%f %f", xx+i, yy+i);
printf("\nSize factor (1.0 = normal size) :");
scanf("%f", &sizefactor);
xx[nmodel] = 1.0; /* Other array elements initialized to 0 */
initgr();
if (k < 3)
{ xmargin = 0.5*(x_max-sizefactor*(x_max-1));
  side(xmargin, 0.5 * y_max, x_max - xmargin, 0.5 * y_max, n);
} else
{ xC = x_max/2; yC = y_max/2;
  r = 0.9 * yC * sizefactor;
  pi = 4 * atan(1.0);
  theta = 2 * pi / k; phi = -0.5 * theta;
  x1 = xC + r * cos(phi); y1 = yC + r * sin(phi);
  for (i=0; i<k; i++)
  { x = x1; y = y1;
    phi += theta;
    x1 = xC + r * cos(phi);
    y1 = yC + r * sin(phi);
    side(x, y, x1, y1, n);
  }
}
endgr();
}
```

We can use program FRCURVE to produce many other interesting figures. For example, if we enter the following seven number pairs x- and y-coordinates of seven model points on the unit interval, we obtain Fig. 4.18 (that is, with recursion depth 3) which is known as the *fractal of Minkowski*:

```
0.25    0
0.25    0.25
0.5     0.25
0.5     0
0.5     -0.25
0.75    -0.25
0.75    0
```

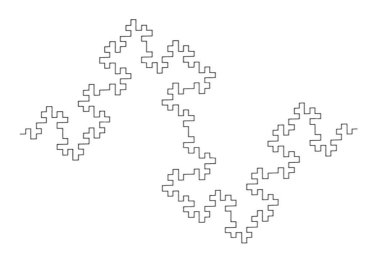

Fig. 4.18. Fractal of Minkowski

Note that the best results are obtained if the line segments that connect our model points (including the end points A and B of the unit interval) are all of the same length, as is indeed the case in our previous example (where this length is 0.25). This is also true if we use the three vertices of an equilateral triangle (with sides of length 1/3) whose base lies in the middle of the unit interval. If we use a (large) square as a base figure, then there are two ways of placing the (small) model triangles on the sides of the square: they will point either outward or inward, as Figs 4.19 and 4.20 show.

With recursion depth $n = 4$ (instead of 1 in Figs 4.19 and 4.20) we obtain Figs 4.21 and 4.22, known as Von Koch curves.

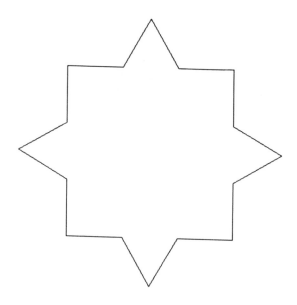

Fig. 4.19. Model triangles pointing outward

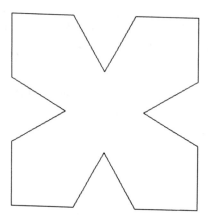

Fig. 4.20. Model triangles pointing inward

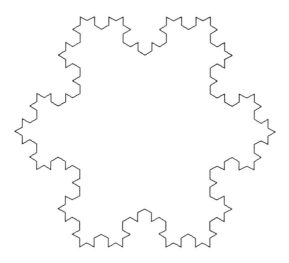

Fig. 4.21. Von Koch curve, based on a triangle and pointing outward

Fig. 4.22. Von Koch curve, based on a triangle and pointing inward

CHAPTER 5

Interactive Graphics

5.1 GRAPHICS INPUT FROM A MOUSE

Besides dealing with graphics output we should also pay some attention to graphics input. Among graphics input devices, the mouse is no doubt the most popular. Many people know how to use a mouse in connection with their favorite software packages, but relatively few programmers know how to use it as an input device in their own programs. Mouse user manuals usually offer too much information on the one hand and too little on the other. You normally find a quite impressive list of your particular mouse's special features (often expressed in both Assembly language and Basic), whereas we are mainly interested in manufacturer-independent characteristics.

After starting up your computer, you have to install the mouse driver if that is not done automatically. For example, if you have a mouse driver in the form of the file MOUSE.COM, and you want to install the driver only when you need it, you can enter the following line to do this:

```
MOUSE
```

The usual way of installing a mouse driver each time the system is started up (regardless of whether it will actually be used) is to include the line

```
DEVICE=MOUSE.SYS
```

in the CONFIG.SYS file. With either method, the mouse driver is placed in memory and its start address is placed at address $51 \times 4 = 204$, which corresponds to interrupt vector 51 (hex. 0x33). You will find this number, 51, in the following two functions, through which we will communicate with the mouse driver, which in turn communicates with the mouse itself:

```
#include <dos.h>
union REGS regs;

int msinit(int Xlo, int Xhi, int Ylo, int Yhi)
{ int retcode;
  regs.x.ax = 0;
  int86(51, &regs, &regs);
  retcode = regs.x.ax;
  /* -1: installed; 0: not installed */
  if (retcode == 0) return 0;
  regs.x.ax = 7;
  regs.x.cx = Xlo; regs.x.dx = Xhi;
  int86(51, &regs, &regs);
  regs.x.ax = 8;
  regs.x.cx = Ylo; regs.x.dx = Yhi;
  int86(51, &regs, &regs);
  return retcode;
}

void msget(int *pX, int *pY, int *pbuttons)
{ regs.x.ax = 3;
  int86(51, &regs, &regs);
  *pX = regs.x.cx; *pY = regs.x.dx);
  *pbuttons = regs.x.bx;
}
```

The type *union REGS* is defined in the header file DOS.H. With our variable *regs* of this type, we simulate the use of the machine registers AX, BX, CX, DX. An Assembly language programmer can use these registers before and after performing the 'software interrupt', for which in this case he or she would write

```
INT 51
```

Instead, we call the function *int86*, declared in DOS.H as

```
int int86(int intno, union REGS *inregs, union REGS *outregs);
```

The parameters, *intno*, *inregs*, *outregs* denote the interrupt number, the registers before the call, and the registers after the call, respectively. Although we will be using several operations (called 'functions' in the mouse manual) the interrupt number to be used for the mouse is always 51. Instead of using various interrupt numbers, we have to place a code for the particular operation to be performed in register AX, that is, in the variable *regs.x.ax*. Our functions *msinit* and *msget* use four such codes, namely:

0:      Reset mouse driver and get status
7:      Set boundaries for x
8:      Set boundaries for y
3:      Read position and button state

We normally call the function *msinit* only once, at the beginning. Then the function *msget* will be called many times, as we will see shortly. With variables X, Y, and *button*, of type *int*, the call

```
msget(&X, &Y, &buttons)
```

will place the current x- and y-values in the variables X and Y, and a non-zero value in *buttons* if a button on the mouse is pressed. Obviously, this makes sense only if there is some coordinate system with minimum and maximum values for X and Y. If in function *msinit* we perform only the first call to *int86* (omitting those with codes 7 and 8 in *regs.x.ax*) then with my mouse the following default values apply to X and Y:

X: 0, 8, 16, ..., 632
Y: 0, 8, 16, ..., 192

Thus by default the coordinate ranges are based on the color graphics adapter, with resolution 640×200, and the step size is 8. (The actual maximum values 639 and 199 for X and Y are rounded down to multiples of 8, which explains the values 632 and 192.) It will now also be clear why the first X and Y values, obtained by *msget* before any mouse movement, are 320 and 100, respectively: these values correspond to the point in the middle of the screen with CGA. With step size 8, the Y ranging from 0 through 192 would mean that there are only 25 different vertical positions, which is not very many. Even with a higher resolution, such as 720×348 for HGA, we sometimes need a smaller step size than 8. Thus, we feel that both a greater number of steps and larger maximum values for X and Y are needed. Fortunately, this effect can be achieved in a simple way, without actually altering the step size.

Let us assume that we want exactly the same number of values for X and Y as there are screen pixels on a horizontal and a vertical line, respectively, and that, as usual, these numbers are $X\_max + 1$ and $Y\_max + 1$. Then we can use the following call:

```
msinit(0, 8 * X_max, 0, 8 * Y_max);
```

Then, after each call to *msget*, we can simply divide the returned X and Y values by 8 to obtain the pixel coordinates as we want them. The results thus obtained can be used to move a *cursor* (also called a *locator*) on the screen, according to our mouse movements. However, it is not necessary to associate mouse

movements with graphics output. In our first program we will therefore simply
display the coordinates derived from mouse movements in digital form.

There is a problem with input from a mouse which should not be overlooked. We
could, of course, program a simple loop, in which we call *msget* to see what the
coordinates are, but, unfortunately, this would produce a very long list with
identical values repeated many times. What we actually want is a function which
returns values X and Y (or the button state) only if there is something new to be
reported. This means that we have to use a wait loop, which terminates as soon
as X, Y, or the button state changes. However, doing this in a straightforward way
would cause another problem: we may want to perform an action as soon as a
key of the keyboard is pressed, and the machine would not listen to any request
of the keyboard if it were waiting only for changes in the state of the mouse. We
therefore have to insert a call to the standard function *kbhit* in the wait loop, as
shown in function *msread*, which can be considered to be at a higher level than
msget:

```
int msread(int *pX, int *pY, int *pbuttons)
{ static int X0=-1, Y0=-1, but0=-1;
  do
  { if (kbhit()) return getch();
    msget(pX, pY, pbuttons);
  } while (*pX == X0 && *pY == Y0 && *pbuttons == but0);
  X0 = *pX; Y0 = *pY; but0 = *pbuttons;
  return -1;
}
```

Program MSDEMO1 uses the functions we have been discussing. It displays the
X and Y coordinates read from the mouse and divided by 8 to obtain pixel
coordinates 0, 1, 2, ... The screen will change only if you either move the mouse
or press any of its buttons. With the Genius mouse the values associated with the
three buttons, from left to right, are 1, 4, 2; the value of 0 is obtained if no
button is being pressed.

```
/* MSDEMO1.C: Demonstration of a mouse as an input device.
*/
#include <conio.h>
#include <stdio.h>
#include <dos.h>
union REGS regs;

int msinit(int Xlo, int Xhi, int Ylo, int Yhi)
{ int retcode;
  regs.x.ax = 0;
  int86(51, &regs, &regs);
  retcode = regs.x.ax;
```

```
  /* -1: installed; 0: not installed */
  if (retcode == 0) return 0;
  regs.x.ax = 7; regs.x.cx = Xlo; regs.x.dx = Xhi;
  int86(51, &regs, &regs);
  regs.x.ax = 8; regs.x.cx = Ylo; regs.x.dx = Yhi;
  int86(51, &regs, &regs);
  return retcode;
}

void msget(int *pX, int *pY, int *pbuttons)
{ regs.x.ax = 3;
  int86(51, &regs, &regs);
  *pX = regs.x.cx; *pY = regs.x.dx;
  *pbuttons = regs.x.bx;
}

int msread(int *pX, int *pY, int *pbuttons)
{ static int X0=-1, Y0=-1, but0=-1;
  do
  { if (kbhit()) return getch();
    msget(pX, pY, pbuttons);
  } while (*pX == X0 && *pY == Y0 && *pbuttons == but0);
  X0 = *pX; Y0 = *pY; but0 = *pbuttons;
  return -1;
}

main()
{ int buttons, X, Y, X_max=719, Y_max=347;  /* HGA */
  printf("This program assumes that a mouse driver is present.\n");
  printf("If so, moving the mouse or pressing any of its buttons\n");
  printf("will display the X and Y coordinates and the button state.\n";;
  printf("You can stop program execution by pressing any key.\n\n");
  if (msinit(0, 8 * X_max, 0, 8 * Y_max) == 0)
  { printf("Mouse or mouse driver not installed.\n"); exit(1);
  }
  while (1)
  { if (msread(&X, &Y, &buttons) >= 0) break;
    printf("buttons =%2d    X=%5d    Y=%5d\n", buttons, X/8, Y/8);
  }
}
```

This program defines X_max and Y_max as values that apply to HGA. If you have a different graphics adapter, then you should change these values. Of course, we need not really do this in practical programs, because we normally use a mouse only when in graphics mode, and our graphics module GRASPTC and the corresponding header file will ensure that the variables X_max and Y_max are available and have their correct values after we have called *initgr*.

5.2 AN INTERACTIVE DEMONSTRATION PROGRAM

Now that we know how to obtain input data read from a mouse we can use this device in our own interactive graphics programs. We will discuss such a program, MSDEMO2, which shows how to program a mouse that moves a cursor on the screen. This program will prepare us for understanding a much larger one, SDRAW, listed and discussed in Section 5.6. Program MSDEMO2 is not really a practical program, but it is very instructive. We can use it not only to move a cursor but also to draw lines, either by mouse control or by entering the coordinates of their end points on the keyboard. Using the mouse, we can draw a line in four steps:

(i)   Move the cursor to one end point of the line to be drawn.
(ii)   Press a mouse button.
(iii)   Move the cursor to the other end point.
(iv)   Release the mouse button.

For the cursor to move reasonably quickly it is necessary that cursor steps caused by mouse movements are larger than one pixel. On the other hand, we want to be able to reach any pixel with the cursor. These two requirements seem contradictory; we will solve this problem by offering the possibility of using very small cursor steps by pressing the arrow keys. Thus, the above steps (i) and (iii) are extended by the option of using the four arrow keys for very fine adjustments.

We will also use coordinates which, as usual, have the following advantages over pixel coordinates:

-   The real length (say, in inches) of a unit does not depend on whether we measure horizontally or vertically.
-   The y-axis points upward.

This new coordinate system is based on the global floating-point variables x_max and y_max. (Recall that $x\_max = 10.0$ and $y\_max \approx 7.0$; see also Section 1.5.) We will actually use integer variables x and y, with maximum values x_max200 and y_max200 which are computed as follows:

```
x_max200 = 200 * x_max;
y_max200 = 200 * y_max;
```

These values are used in the call to the function *msinit*, which we have also been using in the preceding section. Since the mouse yields coordinate values that lie eight units apart, we have $200 \times 10.0/8 - 1 = 249$ steps in the horizontal direction. This was found to be quite reasonable (whereas with the values 100 and 1000 instead of 200 the step size was less adequate). As we will eventually use the new coordinates in HP-GL instructions, we will use the letters HPG of the file-name extension involved to distinguish our new coordinates x and y from the pixel coordinates X and Y. We will use the latter coordinate type for graphics output on the screen; it will therefore be very convenient to have a set of functions for the conversion of HPG-coordinates to pixel coordinates and vice versa. They should be as fast as possible; we will therefore not perform any floating-point computations in them. Starting with a given HPG-coordinate x, we have to multiply it by the quotient

$$\frac{X\_\_max}{x\_max200}$$

to obtain the corresponding pixel coordinate. Instead of using this quotient as a floating-point number, we first multiply x by $X\_\_max$, and then divide it by x_max200. The normal *int* type does not admit the large values that we need for the product, so we have to use type *long int*. With the declarations

```
long x_max200, y_max200;
```

the following conversion functions *Xpixel* and *Ypixel* take HPG-coordinates x and y as arguments and compute pixel coordinates X and Y, whereas the inverse functions *xhpg* and *yhpg* take pixel coordinates X and Y as arguments to compute HPG-coordinates x and y:

```
int Xpixel(int x)
{ return (int)((long)X__max * x / x_max200);
}

int xhpg(int X)
{ return (int)(X * x_max200 / X__max);
}

int Ypixel(int y)
{ return Y__max - (int)((long)Y__max * y / y_max200);
}

int yhpg(int Y)
{ return (int)((Y__max - Y) * y_max200 / Y__max);
}
```

It is a good exercise to verify the following special cases:

```
Xpixel(0) = 0            Xpixel(x_max200) = X__max
xhpg(0)   = 0            xhpg(X__max)     = x_max200

Ypixel(0) = Y__max       Ypixel(y_max200) = 0
yhpg(0)   = y_max200     yhpg(Y__max)     = 0
```

The smallest step made by a mouse is eight units in the HPG-coordinates x and y. As these coordinates have a much wider range than the pixel coordinates X and Y, the step size of eight units is not very large. However, sometimes we may want to reach points in between the 'grid points'; in other words, we may want to place the cursor at points whose HPG-coordinates are not multiples of 8. In these cases we can use the four arrow keys. For example, by pressing the key 'Arrow Right' once, the cursor theoretically moves one HPG-unit to the right. Actually, the cursor may then not move at all, because the video display screen has a rather low resolution so that, due to rounding-off errors, we have either

```
Xpixel(x+1) = Xpixel(x)              or
Xpixel(x+1) = Xpixel(x) + 1
```

Thus, we normally have to press the 'Arrow Right' key more than once to see the cursor really move one pixel to the right, and the same applies to cursor movements in other directions. We will implement this idea by introducing *correction terms* for x and y, which are normally zero but will be positive or negative after we have pressed an arrow key. These correction terms will be algebraically added to the xm and ym coordinates yielded by the mouse, so we will always compute the coordinates x and y of the cursor

$$x = xm + xcorr$$
$$y = ym + ycorr$$

where xm and ym are multiples of 8, and where $xcorr$ and $ycorr$ are zero as long as no arrow keys have been pressed.

In addition to speed, there is another reason for using a step size of as many as eight units. The (invisible) *grid points* with coordinates that are multiples of 8 make it easy to draw lines that are exactly horizontal and vertical and to place the cursor at some point that we have defined previously. Now suppose that as a result of our pressing some arrow keys the variables $xcorr$ and $ycorr$ are non-zero (and that they are not multiples of 8 either). If we then proceed with using only the mouse, the coordinates x and y will not be multiples of 8, which implies that the cursor will not visit the original grid points but rather a set of new ones, which lie $xcorr$ units to the right and $ycorr$ units above the original points. This may be exactly what we want, but sooner or later we may want to revert to the original set of grid points. We will realize this by means of the Home-key. Pressing this key will simply reset $xcorr$ and $ycorr$ to zero, which gives a new position with coordinates $x = xm$, $y = ym$ for the cursor.

In order to see the HPG-coordinate system in action we will also offer the possibility of entering the coordinates x_1, y_1 and x_2, y_2 of the two end points P_1 and P_2 of a line segment that is to be drawn. This method of drawing lines is very general and precise, but it requires much preparation.

Figure 5.1 is a result obtained by running program MSDEMO2. I made the sketch of a tree and my initials in the lower-right corner by means of mouse movements, and used the following lines of text to draw the surrounding square:

```
 100  300     1000  300
1000  300     1000 1200
1000 1200      100 1200
 100 1200      100  300
```

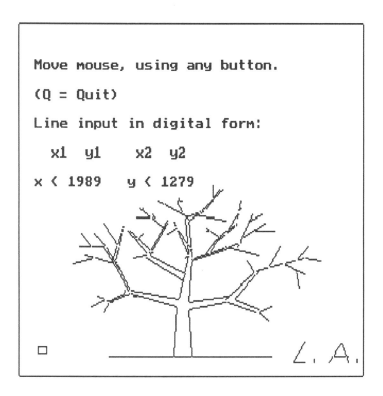

Fig. 5.1. Sample MSDEMO2 screen

The most essential part in program MSDEMO2 is the do-while-loop in the function *main*. As long as we do not press any mouse button, the variable *buttons* will be zero. The function *newposition*, called in this loop, calls the function *cursor* twice: first it erases the existing cursor and then draws a new one. Note that *newposition* returns both the HPG-coordinates x, y, and the pixel coordinates X, Y, through its parameters. As soon as a button is pressed, the variable *buttons* will be non-zero, which causes the function *getline* to be called. At this moment, one end point, say, A, of the line to be drawn is known, and the coordinates of this point are passed to *getline* through parameters. In function *getline*, any new cursor position, found while a mouse button is pressed down, is interpreted as a candidate for the other end point, B, of the line to be drawn. Moving the mouse at this stage implies moving point B, while point A is fixed. Then line AB is drawn, both before and after B is moved, which causes the old line AB to be erased and a new one to be drawn. Thus, we 'drag' point B to where we want it to be, each time displaying not only the current position of B but also the corresponding line AB. Only after releasing the mouse button will AB remain as it is. I hope you will find some more interesting programming details in the following program text.

```
/* MSDEMO2:
       A demonstration program for line drawing
       (intended as a preparation for program
       SDRAW, see Section 5.6.).
*/
#include <conio.h>
#include <dos.h>
#include <stdio.h>
#include <stdlib.h>
#include <ctype.h>

#include "grasptc.h"

union REGS regs;

int Xpixel(int x), Ypixel(int y), xhpg(int X), yhpg(int Y);
int msinit(int Xlo, int Xhi, int Ylo, int Yhi);
int msread(int *pX, int *pY, int *pbuttons);
void getline(int *pxstart, int *pystart);
void drline(int x1, int y1, int x2, int y2);
void digitalline(char ch);
void cursor(int X, int Y);
void newposition(int *px, int *py, int *pX, int *pY, int *pbut);

long x_max200, y_max200;
int y200, xmin, xmax, ymin, ymax, Xmin, Xmax, Ymin, Ymax;

#define txt(linenr, str) gotoxy(1, linenr); cprintf(str);

main()
{ int buttons, xm, ym, X, Y, x, y;
  char str[100];
  clrscr();
  txt(1, "This program requires a mouse driver to be present.");
  txt(4, "You can draw straight lines as follows:");
  txt(5, "Move the cursor to one end point of the line, then press");
```

```
txt(6, "a mouse button, and move the cursor to the other end point");
txt(7, "of the line. Finally, release the mouse button.");
txt(9, "Normally, the cursor can only be placed at grid points");
txt(10, "that horizontally and vertically lie eight units apart.");
txt(11, "If you want the cursor to move very small distances, use");
txt(12, "the four arrow keys. Press the Home-key if and when you");
txt(13, "want the cursor to go back to a grid point.");
txt(15, "You can also draw a line by entering four numbers, namely");
txt(16, "the two coordinate pairs x1, y1, x2, y2 of its end points.");
txt(18, "Press any key on the keyboard to start the demonstration.");
if (getch() == 3) exit(0); /* 3 = Ctrl-C */
initgr();
outtextxy(50, 50, "Move mouse, using any button.");
outtextxy(50, 70, "(Q = Quit)");
x_max200 = 200 * x_max; y_max200 = y200 = 200 * y_max;
Xmin = 4; Xmax = X__max - 4;
Ymin = 2; Ymax = Y__max - 12;
xmax = xhpg(Xmax); ymax = yhpg(Ymin);
xmin = xhpg(Xmin); ymin = yhpg(Ymax);
outtextxy(50, 90, "Line input in digital form:");
outtextxy(50, 110, "  x1  y1    x2  y2");
sprintf(str, "x < %d   y < %d", xmax+1, ymax+1);
outtextxy(50, 130, str);
setwritemode(XOR_PUT);

if (msinit(0, (int)x_max200, 0, (int)y_max200) == 0)
{ to_text();
  cprintf("No mouse or mouse driver"); exit(1);
}
while (msread(&xm, &ym, &buttons) >= 0) ;
  /* Read xm and ym and skip any keyboard input. */
x = xm; y = ym; cursor(x, y);

for ( ; ; )    /* Main program loop */
{ newposition(&x, &y, &X, &Y, &buttons);
  if (buttons) getline(&x, &y);
}
}


/* Functions in alphabetic order:
*/

void cursor(int x, int y)
{ int Xm4, Ym2, Ym1, Xp4, Yp2, Yp1, X, Y;
  X = Xpixel(x); Y = Ypixel(y);
  Xm4=X-4; Xp4=X+4; Ym2=Y-2; Ym1=Y-1; Yp1=Y+1; Yp2=Y+2;
  line(Xm4, Ym2, Xp4, Ym2); line(Xm4, Yp2, Xp4, Yp2);
```

```c
    line(Xm4, Ym1, Xm4, Yp1); line(Xp4, Ym1, Xp4, Yp1);
}

void digitalline(char ch)
{ int x1, y1, x2, y2, i=0;
  char str[100];
  do
  { str[i++] = ch; ch = getch();
  } while (ch != '\n' && ch != '\r');
  str[i] = '\0';
  if (sscanf(str, "%d %d %d %d", &x1, &y1, &x2, &y2) < 4) return;
  drline(x1, y1, x2, y2);
}

void getline(int *pxstart, int *pystart)
{ int x, y, xstart, ystart, buttons, x0, y0, X, Y;
  x = xstart = *pxstart; X = Xpixel(x);
  y = ystart = *pystart; Y = Ypixel(y);
  do
  { x0 = x; y0 = y;
    newposition(&x, &y, &X, &Y, &buttons);
    if (x != x0 || y != y0)
    { drline(xstart, ystart, x0, y0);    /* Erase */
      drline(xstart, ystart, x, y);      /* Drag  */
    }
  } while (buttons);
  *pxstart=x; *pystart=y;
}

void drline(int x1, int y1, int x2, int y2)
{ int X1, Y1, X2, Y2;
  X1 = Xpixel(x1); Y1 = Ypixel(y1);
  X2 = Xpixel(x2); Y2 = Ypixel(y2);
  if (X1 == X2 && Y1 == Y2) return;
  line(X1, Y1, X2, Y2);
}

void endprogram(void)
{ to_text(); exit(0);
}

int msinit(int Xlo, int Xhi, int Ylo, int Yhi)
{ int retcode;
  regs.x.ax = 0; int86(51, &regs, &regs);
  retcode = regs.x.ax;
    /* -1: installed; 0: not installed */
  if (retcode == 0) return 0;
  regs.x.ax = 7; regs.x.cx = Xlo; regs.x.dx = Xhi;
```

```c
    int86(51, &regs, &regs);
    regs.x.ax = 8; regs.x.cx = Ylo; regs.x.dx = Yhi;
    int86(51, &regs, &regs);
    return retcode;
}

int msread(int *px, int *py, int *pbuttons)
{ static int x0=-10000, y0, but0;
  int xnew, ynew;
  do
  { if (kbhit()) return getch();
    regs.x.ax = 3; int86(51, &regs, &regs);
    xnew = regs.x.cx; ynew = regs.x.dx;
    *pbuttons = regs.x.bx;
  } while (xnew == x0 && ynew == y0 && *pbuttons == but0);
  *px = xnew; *py = y200 - ynew;.
  x0 = xnew; y0 = ynew; but0 = *pbuttons;
  return -1;
}

void newposition(int *px, int *py, int *pX, int *pY, int *pbut)
{ int ch, x0=*px, y0=*py, x, y;
  static int xm, ym, xcorr=0, ycorr=0;
  ch = msread(&xm, &ym, pbut); ch = tolower(ch);
  if (ch >= 0)
  { if (ch == 0)
    { ch = getch();
      switch (ch)
      { case 72: ycorr++; break; /* Up     */
        case 75: xcorr--; break; /* Left   */
        case 77: xcorr++; break; /* Right  */
        case 80: ycorr--; break; /* Down   */
        case 71: xcorr = ycorr = 0; break;
                                 /* Home   */
      }
    }
  }
  if (ch == 'q') endprogram(); else
  if (isdigit(ch)) digitalline(ch);
  x = xm + xcorr; y = ym + ycorr;
  if (x < xmin) x = xmin;
  if (x > xmax) x = xmax;
  if (y < ymin) y = ymin;
  if (y > ymax) y = ymax;
  if (x != x0 || y != y0)
  { cursor(x0, y0);    /* Erase   */
    cursor(x, y);      /* Display */
  }
```

```
  *px = x; *py = y;
  *pX = Xpixel(x); *pY = Ypixel(y);
}

int xhpg(int X)
{ return (int)(X * x_max200 / X__max);
}

int Xpixel(int x)
{ return (int)((long)X__max * x / x_max200);
}

int yhpg(int Y)
{ return (int)((Y__max - Y) * y_max200 / Y__max);
}

int Ypixel(int y)
{ return Y__max - (int)((long)Y__max * y / y_max200);
}
```

5.3 VIEWPORTS AND IMAGES

Viewports

In Turbo C we can define a *viewport*, which is a rectangle (with a horizontal side)
in which we display graphics output. As we already know how to display graphics
output anywhere on the screen, you may wonder if we really need this concept.
Now suppose that in the graphics mode we have displayed some lines of text on
the screen and we want to replace them with different text. Curiously enough,
without special procedures the old text will not disappear when the new text is
written on top of it, so the new and the old text will be at the same place, which,
of course, results in confusion. We therefore have to clear the area occupied by
the old text before writing the new text, and an efficient way of doing this is
clearing some viewport which contains the old text. At any time, there is only one
current viewport, and all (pixel-) coordinates are relative to it. By default, the
current viewport consists of the full screen. Here are the declarations of some
Turbo C functions that deal with viewports:

```
  void far setviewport(int left, int top, int right, int bottom,
                       int clipflag);
  void far clearviewport(void);
  void far getviewsettings(struct viewporttype far *viewport);
```

Type *struct viewporttype*, occurring in the last function prototype, is defined in the header file GRAPHICS.H as follows:

```
struct viewporttype
{ int left, top, right, bottom;
  int clipflag;
}
```

Let us now see how to solve the problem about replacing text, mentioned above. The following function can be used to clear any rectangle (with a horizontal side) on the screen:

```
void clearrectangle(int Xtop, int Ytop, int Xbottom, int Ybottom)
{ struct viewporttype vp;
  getviewsettings(&vp);
  setviewport(Xtop, Ytop, Xbottom, Ybottom, 0);
  clearviewport();
  setviewport(vp.left, vp.top, vp.right, vp.bottom, vp.clip);
}
```

In this function, we first use *getviewsettings* to retrieve information about the current viewport (which may be the full screen), and to store it in the local variable *vp*. Then we define a new viewport, with $(Xtop, Ytop)$ as its upper-left and $(Xbottom, Ybottom)$ as its lower-right corner, merely to clear it by means of the subsequent call to *clearviewport*. Finally, we restore the original viewport settings, using the data stored in the local variable *vp*. We can use *clearrectangle* in, for example, the following function, which displays a line of text at the bottom of the screen, replacing any previous text. It uses the global variables $X\_\_max$ and $Y\_\_max$, declared in GRASPTC.H and assigned their proper values (*getmaxx()* and *getmaxy()*, respectively) in our function *initgr*.

```
void displaybotlin(char *str)
{ clearrectangle(1, Y__max-10, X__max-1, Y__max-1);
  outtextxy(4, Y__max-10, str);
}
```

Note that clearing a rectangle in this function does not affect any lines at the very edges of the screen, which could have been drawn, for example, by

```
rectangle(0, 0, X__max, Y__max);
```

In our first call to *setviewport* we have used *clipflag* = 0. If we use a viewport to draw lines in it, then with *clipflag* = 1 those lines are clipped against the edges of the viewport: if only a part of a line lies inside the viewport, only that part is drawn. With *clipflag* = 0, the result is undefined in those cases.

It should be remembered that pixel coordinates in graphics output functions are always relative to the current viewport. This means that as far as displaying text on the bottom of the screen is concerned, we could have used the single function

```
void displaybotlin1(char *str)
{ struct viewporttype vp;
  getviewsettings(&vp);
  setviewport(1, Y__max-10, X_max-1, Y_max-1, 0);
  clearviewport();
  outtextxy(3, 0, str);
  setviewport(vp.left, vp.top, vp.right, vp.bottom, vp.clip);
}
```

instead of the two functions *displaybotlin* and *clearrectangle*. Note the pixel coordinates $X = 3$ and $Y = 0$, used in the call to *outtextxy*. These are relative to the viewport just defined. The function *setviewport* itself is not a graphics output function and therefore takes absolute pixel coordinates, not depending on the current viewport. We need function *clearrectangle* in any case because it is also useful for other purposes. We will therefore actually use *displaybotlin* rather than *displaybotlin1*.

Images

There are three extremely useful functions in Turbo C to read an image (similar to the contents of a viewport) from the screen into memory and to write it to the screen later. These are declared in GRAPHICS.H as follows:

```
unsigned far imagesize(int left, int top, int right, int bottom);
void far getimage(int left, int top, int right, int bottom,
                  void far *bitmap);
void far putimage(int left, int top, void far *bitmap, int op);
```

Before using *getimage*, we can inquire how many bytes this function will need; we only have to call *imagesize* for this. For example, let us assume that we have some graphics result on the screen, part of which is temporarily to be replaced with some message (in the string *str*), which fits in one line, say, in the middle of the screen. On the next line the message

```
Press any key...
```

is to appear. As soon as a key is pressed, the original graphics results are to be restored. The following program, IMAGE, which, as usual, is to be linked together with our graphics module GRASPTC, contains the function *message*, which does all this.

```
/* IMAGE: This program demonstrates the Turbo C functions
          imagesize, getimage, and putimage.
*/

#include <alloc.h>
#include <conio.h>
#include "grasptc.h"

void clearrectangle(int Xtop, int Ytop, int Xbottom, int Ybottom)
{ struct viewporttype vp;
  getviewsettings(&vp);
  setviewport(Xtop, Ytop, Xbottom, Ybottom, 0);
  clearviewport();
  setviewport(vp.left, vp.top, vp.right, vp.bottom, vp.clip);
}

void message(char *str)
{ char *buffer;
  int xC=X__max/2, yC=Y__max/2, left, right, top, bottom, h, w, w1;
  h = textheight("A");
  top = yC - 2 * h;
  bottom = yC + 2 * h;
  w = textwidth(str);
  w1 = textwidth("Press any key...");
  if (w1 > w) w = w1;
  w += 16;
  left = xC - w/2; right = xC + w/2;
  buffer = farmalloc(imagesize(left, top, right, bottom));
  if (buffer == NULL) {outtextxy(xC, yC, "Not enough memory"); return;}
  getimage(left, top, right, bottom, buffer);
  clearrectangle(left, top, right, bottom);
  settextjustify(CENTER_TEXT, CENTER_TEXT);
  outtextxy(xC, yC-h-h/4, str);
  outtextxy(xC, yC+h, "Press any key...");
  getch();
  putimage(left, top, buffer, COPY_PUT);
  farfree(buffer);
}

#define N 20

main()
{ int xC, yC, i, xstep, ystep;
  initgr();
  xC=X__max/2; yC=Y__max/2; xstep = xC/N; ystep = yC/N;
  for (i=1; i<=N; i++) ellipse(xC, yC, 0, 360, i*xstep, i*ystep);
  message("This is just an example of how text"
          " can temporarily overwrite graphics.");
```

```
    message("Once again.");
    endgr();
}
```

The main program draws a set of 20 concentric ellipses, and, when they are completed, it displays two lines of text in the middle of the screen, as Fig. 5.2 shows. When we press a key, as requested, then the text in the middle of the screen is replaced with

```
            Once again.
            Press any key...
```

Since the first of these two lines takes less room than the first line in Fig. 5.2, many of the original ellipses can be restored, and this is what happens. When we press a key again, even all the original ellipses are restored. As usual, we finally have to press a key to switch back to text mode and to terminate the program. (Actually, Fig. 5.2 was made with a slightly different version of program IMAGE, as we will see in the next section.)

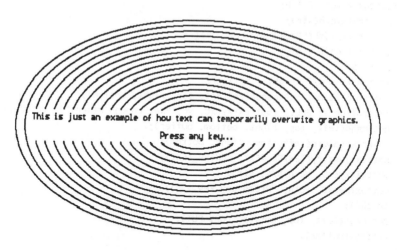

Fig. 5.2. Text replacing a saved image

We have not yet discussed the fourth parameter, *op*, of *putimage*. This denotes an operation for which the following possibilities are available:

Name	Value
COPY_PUT	0
XOR_PUT	1
OR_PUT	2
AND_PUT	3
NOT_PUT	4

Normally, we use *COPY_PUT*, as we did here; in this way the saved image simply overwrites what is on the screen. We associate each pixel that has the foreground color with a 1-bit and each pixel that has the background color with a 0-bit in screen memory. With *XOR_PUT*, all bits of the saved image are 'exclusively ORed' with the corresponding bits of the image on the screen. The effect is that only the subset of the pixels that correspond with 1-bits in the saved image are inverted. With *OR_PUT*, those pixels are not inverted but given the foreground color, and with *AND_PUT* the selected pixels will have the foreground color only if they already have that color; otherwise they will have the background color. Besides *COPY_PUT*, the values *OR_PUT* and *NOT_PUT* also have very useful applications, as the following sections will show.

5.4 MAKING LINES FATTER

Frequently we want to include the contents of the entire graphics computer screen in a report or a book. As discussed in Chapter 3, if we have to use bit-mapped graphics there may be a problem if the image on the screen is much larger than the picture that we eventually want. Although desktop publishing packages such as Ventura Publisher and WordPerfect enable us to reduce the image to the desired size, this does not always solve our problem, since thin lines (and thin characters) may disappear when they are reduced. We may therefore want to make both lines and characters fatter before we make a screen capture. If we have only lines drawn in our program, the best way to overcome this difficulty is to use the Turbo C function *setlinestyle*, discussed in Section 2.8, to make lines three pixels wide. However, that function does not affect other pixels, such as those of characters. The following function performs the task of making lines, characters and any other objects fatter. It is based on the assumption that (with monochrome graphics) the foreground color has been used for thin objects which may be made fatter at the expense of pixels in the background color.

```
/* FATTER: This function makes on-screen lines
           and characters fatter.
*/
#include <alloc.h>
#include "grasptc.h"
```

```
void fatter(void)
{ char *buf;
  buf = farmalloc(imagesize(0, 0, X__max-1, Y__max-1));
  if (buf == NULL)
  { outtextxy(X__max/2, Y__max/2,
      "Not enough memory");
    return;
  }
  getimage(0, 0, X__max-1, Y__max-1, buf);
  putimage(1, 0, buf, OR_PUT);
  putimage(0, 1, buf, OR_PUT);
  putimage(1, 1, buf, OR_PUT);
  farfree(buf);
}
```

This function takes the entire screen contents (except for the column $X = X\_\_max$ and the line $Y = Y\_\_max$) and copies it three times in the following way. For any position (X, Y) of the saved image, it is copied in the positions $(X+1, Y)$, $(X, Y+1)$, and $(X+1, Y+1)$ if it is a 1-bit. If, on the other hand, position (X, Y) is a 0-bit, the three other positions mentioned are left unchanged. As a result, there will no longer be any lines only one pixel wide (possibly except possibly for the right-hand and the bottom edge of the screen).

This method has a drawback: any open space only one pixel wide between two lines will disappear. In practice, normal lines lie wider apart than one pixel, so there seems to be no real problem. However, we have to be very careful with characters. For example, in the default (bit-mapped) font of Turbo C, the open space in the upper part of the small letter 'e' is only one pixel high, so this would disappear. Also, most vertical lines in the default font, such as that at the left of the small letter 'b', is already two pixels wide; as we are going to make such lines fat ourselves, an original width of one pixel would do. With the default font, increasing the character size (using the function *settextstyle*) would make the characters twice as large, which in most cases is more than we want. Fortunately, we can also use stroked fonts, which offer much better facilities in this regard. Among the various stroked fonts, we choose the 'small font', since this gives characters the elementary curves of which are only one pixel wide. Obviously, this can be useful only if we use both enlarged characters and our *fatter* function (otherwise this font would be the worst of all for our purposes). With the Hercules Graphics Adapter (resolution 720 × 348), I found quite satisfactory results with the following function calls:

```
settextstyle(SMALL_FONT, HORIZ_DIR, 0);
setusercharsize(3, 2, 3, 2);
```

As discussed in Section 1.6, the latter function gives us control over the size of text with stroked fonts. We can use it only after a call to *settextstyle* that has 0 as its final argument (*charsize*). In the above call to *setusercharsize*, both the character width and the character height are scaled with the factor 3.0/2.0. I have actually inserted the above two function calls immediately after the call to *initgr* in program IMAGE of Section 5.3, and I also inserted the statement

```
fatter();
```

immediately after the call

```
outtextxy(xC, yC+h, "Press any key...");
```

in function *message* of that program. After the function *fatter* has been called, the call to *getch* causes the computer to wait and, with WordPerfect's GRAB utility in memory, we can now moment press Shift-Alt-F9 and make a screen capture. This is how I made Fig. 5.2. If after this we press another key, as requested on the screen, program execution is resumed, but now the results are not as good as they were with our version that did not call the function *fatter*. Recall that, before displaying the two lines of text in the middle of the ellipses, we have saved the image of the corresponding portion of the screen, using *getimage*, but then the ellipses had not yet been made fat. Consequently, now that we are restoring the original portion of the ellipses, using *putimage*, the elliptic arcs that reappear are still thin, while the remaining arcs are fat. This is why the call to *fatter* appears only in a special version of program IMAGE, not in the program text listed in the previous section.

5.5 MENUS

We will now see how to move the mouse in order to select some item in a menu. For simplicity, we will introduce a menu with only three items, *Item A*, *Item B*, and *Quit*. We will display these three item names in 'boxes', which are rectangles above each other, on the upper-left part of the screen. If we move the cursor to one of these three rectangles and then press a mouse button the item name indicated will appear in the middle of the screen. If it happens to be the name *Quit* then the program will terminate after about 3 seconds. We will also highlight the selected item by displaying its menu box in reverse video: all pixels in the box will be inverted for about 2 seconds. Fig. 5.3 shows the screen after the selection of *Item A*.

The method of producing fat lines by means of *putimage*, as discussed in the previous section, does not work when part of the screen is inverted, as is the case here with the *Item A* box. Remember that with *putimage* and *XOR_PUT* the number of pixels in the foreground color increases. This normally makes lines and characters fatter because they are in the foreground color. However, if the

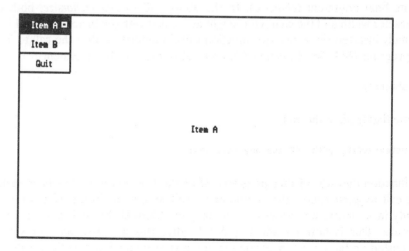

Fig. 5.3. Menu and selected item

pixels of a part of the screen are inverted then in that part the lines and characters are in the background color and the background is displayed in the foreground color. Since our method increases the number of pixels in the foreground color at the expense of those in the background, thin lines and characters in the inverted area would completely disappear instead of being made fat! We will therefore not use the *fatter* function in our menu program, but rather the Turbo C function *setlinestyle* (discussed in Section 2.8) to draw lines three pixels wide. Incidentally, if this function is combined with the call

```
setwritemode(XOR_PUT);
```

thick lines are actually inverted, which we will use to draw and erase the cursor. As for characters, we can again use the 'small font' with scale factors 1.5, as we did in the previous section, but instead of writing the text only once, say, at point (X, Y), we will write it four times, at points (X, Y), $(X+1, Y)$, $(X, Y+1)$, $(X+1, Y+1)$. Although the Turbo C manual does not state this explicitly, the write mode XOR_PUT also applies to stroked fonts, which means that during our displaying text four times in almost identical positions we must temporarily reset the write mode to $COPY\_PUT$. Further programming details can be found in the following program:

```c
/* MENU: A very simple menu.
*/
#include <dos.h>
#include <stdlib.h>
#include <alloc.h>
#include "grasptc.h"

union REGS regs;

int msinit(int Xlo, int Xhi, int Ylo, int Yhi);
void msget(int *pX, int *pY, int *pbuttons);
void msread(int *pX, int *pY, int *pbuttons);
void mouse_cursor(int *pX, int *pY, int *pbut);
void cursor(int X, int Y);
void clearrectangle(int Xtop, int Ytop, int Xbottom, int Ybottom);
void invertbox(int i, int X, int Y);
void outtxtxy1(int X, int Y, char *str);

char *ptr;

#define WIDTH 100
#define HEIGHT 30

main()
{ int buttons, XC, YC, X, Y, i;
  initgr();
  XC = X__max/2; YC = Y__max/2;
  setlinestyle(SOLID_LINE, 0, THICK_WIDTH);
  settextstyle(SMALL_FONT, HORIZ_DIR, 0);
  setusercharsize(3, 2, 3, 2);
  settextjustify(CENTER_TEXT, CENTER_TEXT);
  ptr = farmalloc(imagesize(1, 1, WIDTH-1, HEIGHT-1));
  if (ptr == NULL)
  { outtextxy(XC, YC, "Not enough memory");
    delay(1000); exit(1);
  }
  if (msinit(0, X__max, 0, Y__max) == 0)
  { outtextxy(XC, YC, "Mouse or mouse driver absent");
    delay(1000); exit(1);
  }
  rectangle(1, 1, X__max-1, Y__max-1);
  line(WIDTH, 0, WIDTH, 3*HEIGHT);
  for (i=1; i<=3; i++) line(0, i*HEIGHT+1, WIDTH, i*HEIGHT+1);
  outtxtxy1(WIDTH/2, HEIGHT/2, "Item A");
  outtxtxy1(WIDTH/2, 3*HEIGHT/2, "Item B");
  outtxtxy1(WIDTH/2, 5*HEIGHT/2, "Quit");
  msread(&X, &Y, &buttons);
  setwritemode(XOR_PUT);
```

```
cursor(X, Y);  /* Very first cursor */

do
{ mouse_cursor(&X, &Y, &buttons);
  if (buttons && X < WIDTH && Y < 3*HEIGHT)
  { do mouse_cursor(&X, &Y, &buttons); while (buttons);
     /* Now the button is no longer pressed down! */
    i = Y/HEIGHT;
    invertbox(i, X, Y); /* Highlight selected item */
    clearrectangle(XC-100, YC-20, XC+100, YC+20);
    switch (i)
    { case 0: outtxtxy1(XC, YC, "Item A"); break;
      case 1: outtxtxy1(XC, YC, "Item B"); break;
      case 2: outtxtxy1(XC, YC, "Quit");
              delay(3000); to_text(); exit(0);
    }
    delay(2000);
    invertbox(i, X, Y);
  }
} while (1);
}

void clearrectangle(int Xtop, int Ytop, int Xbottom, int Ybottom)
{ struct viewporttype vp;
  getviewsettings(&vp);
  setviewport(Xtop, Ytop, Xbottom, Ybottom, 0);
  clearviewport();
  setviewport(vp.left, vp.top, vp.right, vp.bottom, vp.clip);
}

void cursor(int X, int Y)
{ line(X-5, Y-3, X+5, Y-3);
  line(X-5, Y+3, X+5, Y+3);
  line(X-4, Y-1, X-4, Y+1);
  line(X+4, Y-1, X+4, Y+1);
}

void invertbox(int i, int x, int y)
{ int ih=i*HEIGHT;
  cursor(x, y); /* Erase */
  getimage(3, ih+3, WIDTH-2, ih+HEIGHT-1, ptr);
  putimage(3, ih+3, ptr, NOT_PUT);
  cursor(x, y); /* Restore */
}



void mouse_cursor(int *pX, int *pY, int *pbut)
```

```
{ int Xold=*pX, Yold=*pY;
  msread(pX, pY, pbut);
  cursor(Xold, Yold);   /* Erase old cursor */
  cursor(*pX, *pY);     /* Draw new cursor  */
}


int msinit(int Xlo, int Xhi, int Ylo, int Yhi)
{ int retcode;
  regs.x.ax = 0;
  int86(51, &regs, &regs);
  retcode = regs.x.ax;
    /* -1: installed; 0: not installed */
  if (retcode == 0) return 0;
  regs.x.ax = 7; regs.x.cx = Xlo; regs.x.dx = Xhi;
  int86(51, &regs, &regs);
  regs.x.ax = 8; regs.x.cx = Ylo; regs.x.dx = Yhi;
  int86(51, &regs, &regs);
  return retcode;
}


void msread(int *px, int *py, int *pbuttons)
{ static int x0=-10000, y0, but0;
  int xnew, ynew;
  do
  { regs.x.ax = 3;
    int86(51, &regs, &regs);
    xnew = regs.x.cx; ynew = regs.x.dx;
    *pbuttons = regs.x.bx;
  } while (xnew == x0 && ynew == y0 &&
           *pbuttons == but0);
  *px = x0 = xnew; *py = y0 = ynew;
  but0 = *pbuttons;
}


void outtxtxy1(int X, int Y, char *str)
{ setwritemode(COPY_PUT);
  outtextxy(X, Y, str);
  outtextxy(X+1, Y, str);
  outtextxy(X, Y+1, str);
  outtextxy(X+1, Y+1, str);
  setwritemode(XOR_PUT);
}
```

5.6 A DRAW PROGRAM

This section is about a simple draw program, SDRAW. We can use it to draw lines, circles, arcs, and arrows and to insert text, provided that a mouse is available. It will be possible to save our drawing in HP-GL format in a file, so that we can import it in, for example, WordPerfect or Ventura Publisher. Also, we can read this 'HPG file' later in program SDRAW itself, which is useful if we want to edit the drawing. We will use menus in which we make selections by moving a cursor (by means of mouse movements) and pressing a button of the mouse. The program cannot compete with commercial draw packages, but it can be used for all kinds of simple drawings, such as Fig. 2.8 in Section 2.4. Unlike professional draw programs, SDRAW is given in source code, so you can modify and extend it in any way. Before discussing some programming aspects of SDRAW, we will see what users can do with it.

User aspects

You can use SDRAW only if you have a mouse and if a mouse driver has been installed. If you then type

```
SDRAW
```

the following initial text screen appears:

```
SDRAW: A program to draw lines, arcs, and text, and to produce
HP-GL files; these files can be read by this very program and
by, for example, WordPerfect 5.0 and Ventura Publisher.

You can draw straight lines as follows:
Move the cursor to one end point of the line, then press
a mouse button, and move the cursor to the other end point.
Finally, release the mouse button.

Normally, the cursor can be placed only at grid points
that horizontally and vertically lie eight units apart.
If you want the cursor to move very small distances, use
the four arrow keys. Press the Home-key to move the cursor
back to the nearest grid point.

For other operations, use the mouse and the menu and follow
the directions displayed on the bottom line.

Press any key on the keyboard...
```

After pressing a key you obtain a graphics screen consisting of three portions:

- The work area, a large empty rectangle.
- The message area at the bottom of the screen, also initially empty.
- The main menu, at the left.

When working with SDRAW, you build a drawing in the work area, and messages may be displayed in the message area, as shown, in Fig. 5.4.

Somewhere on the screen you can see a small square, the *cursor*. Moving the mouse causes the cursor to move in the same direction. Drawing lines is very simple. You only have to place the cursor at one end point, press a button, and move the cursor to the other end point, while keeping the button pressed down. You will see a line like a 'rubber band', connecting the first end point (where you pressed down the mouse button) with the current cursor position. When the cursor has arrived at the desired end point, release the cursor; the rubber band now becomes a fixed line segment. So as long as you are drawing only lines you need not use the menu.

Moving the mouse actually causes the cursor to make small steps of a fixed size. These steps are larger than one pixel, so in this way we can reach only *grid points*: the distance between two neighboring points is equal to the step size. In this way it is not difficult to return to some end point of a line segment, as is necessary, for example, to draw the final side of a triangle (or any other polygon). For many simple sketches the system of grid points is fine enough to use only those points as end points of line segments. But we sometimes want finer control over cursor movements. Then it is normally desirable to display the coordinates of the current cursor position. You can do this by moving the cursor to the box labeled *Coordinates* in the menu area and pressing a mouse button. You will then see the coordinates of the cursor in the message area at the bottom of the screen, as shown in Fig. 5.4. If you move the cursor from the lower-left to the upper-right corner of the screen, both x and y increase, etc. The coordinates are expressed in *plotter units*, which are 200 times as large as our usual user coordinates. These values are actually written to a file, if you use the *Write* option of the menu. Although they are integers (which is required in HP-GL), their range provides a much higher resolution than the pixel-coordinate range. When using the mouse, you will see that the step size is equal to eight plotter units, so in this way all plotter coordinates are multiples of 8. However, you can also reach points with other coordinate values, namely by using the *arrow keys*. For example, by pressing the 'arrow right' key ($\rightarrow$) once, you increase the x-coordinate by one, so if its value was 800, its new value will be 801. If you then move the mouse slowly to the right, the x-coordinate values will be 809, 817, etc., which means that a new system of grid points is now in use. You can return to the old system (with coordinates that are multiples of 8) by pressing the Home key.

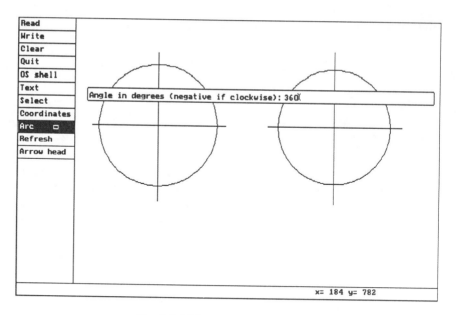

Fig. 5.4. Main menu and dialog box

In general, you select a menu option by moving the cursor to some point inside the menu box for that option and by pressing any mouse button. We will now discuss all menu options shown in Fig. 5.4.

The *Write* and *Read* options can be used to save and retrieve a drawing we have made. The file is in HP-GL format, which means that for each line only the coordinates of the two end points are stored. In its current form SDRAW cannot read an arbitrary HP-GL file but only those that have also been written by SDRAW. Only a small subset of HP-GL is used; this not only keeps the program simple but it also avoids any problems due to restrictions imposed by other programs. For example, WordPerfect accepts only a subset of HP-GL, which includes the subset we are using. Both with *Read* and *Write* you are asked to enter a file name; this is done in a dialog box, similar to that shown in Fig. 5.4 (which we will discuss shortly), but with the following text:

```
File name:
```

Such dialog boxes seem to destroy the drawing you are producing, but after you have satisfactorily answered the question in the box and pressed the Enter key the box and its contents disappear and the original drawing is restored. If you are using the *Read* option and there is no file with the given name, the following message appears in the dialog box:

```
Can't open file; press Esc.
```

Pressing the Escape key will then cause the dialog box to disappear. On the other hand, if you are using *Write* and you enter the name of an existing file, the following text appears in the dialog box:

```
Overwrite existing file? (Y/N):
```

This prevents you from overwriting files by accident.

The *Quit* menu option is to end SDRAW and to return to DOS. If there is a drawing on the screen and we have not yet saved it, we are asked:

```
Save drawing? (Y/N/Esc.):
```

Besides answering *Yes* or *No* (*Y/N*) you can press the Esc key if you do not want to quit, after all. The question of saving our drawing also appears if you select the *Clear* option, which you can use to clear the screen so that you can start with a new drawing.

It is also possible to leave SDRAW temporarily by means of the option *OS shell*. This option causes the normal DOS prompt to appear, followed by the text

```
Type EXIT to return to SDRAW.
```

You can use this, for example, to see what is in your directory by typing *DIR*. When you type *EXIT* the latest SDRAW graphics screen is restored. You should really do this, and not misuse *OS shell* instead of *Quit*; only by leaving SDRAW in the normal way (or by using Ctrl-C or Ctrl-Break!) will its memory space become available for other purposes.

If you want to enter text in your drawing, then, not surprisingly, you have to select the *Text* option. This causes the following text to be displayed in the message area at the bottom of the screen:

```
Move cursor to where text is to begin and press button
```

By doing this, the shape of the cursor changes (into a figure somewhat similar to the letter I), and at the indicated position we are expected to enter text. We can enter only one line of text at a time: pressing the Enter key indicates the end of the text and causes the normal (square) cursor to return. The text shown in Fig. 5.5 was entered in this way. (We will discuss the circles and polygons displayed there shortly.)

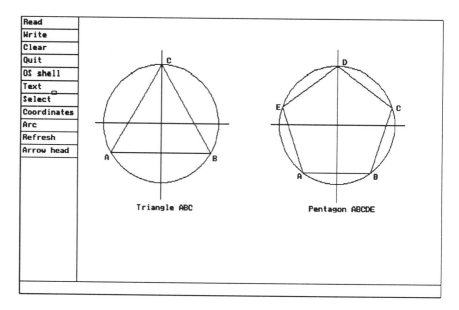

Fig. 5.5. Triangle and pentagon

After using the *Write* command, discussed above, we obtain an HPG file. When we import this in WordPerfect 5.0, we obtain Fig. 5.6. It is interesting to compare Figs 5.5 and 5.6.

To align the start positions of several pieces of text it is often useful to have the cursor coordinates displayed, which, as mentioned previously, is done by selecting the *Coordinate* option. Using that option once again causes the coordinates to disappear from the message area. In that way, the cursor can follow mouse movements more quickly (especially on the slow PC XT that I am using).

When we are drawing we often want to *delete* (or *erase*) some line segments or pieces of text (collectively called *objects*). Similarly, we may want to either *move* or *copy* an object. For each of these three actions the option to use is *Select*. After all, we can delete, move, or copy an object only after selecting it. If we move the cursor to the *Select* box and press a mouse button, the following text is displayed in the message area:

```
Move cursor to selected object and press button.
```

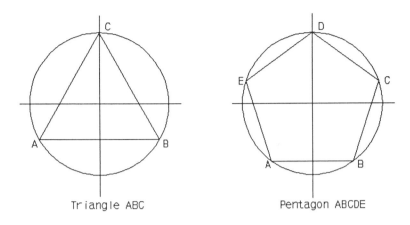

Triangle ABC   Pentagon ABCDE

Fig. 5.6. Resulting drawing, based on HPG file

If the object in question is a line you can select it by placing the cursor anywhere on that line; if it is a string of text you should place it at the start point, that is, in the lower-left corner of its first character. Pressing a button at such a position causes a new menu to appear, as shown in Fig. 5.7. As you can see, this 'secondary menu' overwrites part of the main menu. Also, the message area now reads

```
Select operation.
```

which means that you have to select one of the four options of the secondary menu. Besides *Delete*, *Move*, *Copy*, there is also the *Escape* option, which you can use if, on second thoughts, you don't want to delete, move, or copy anything at all; the secondary menu then disappears immediately and the main menu is restored.

If the selected object is a **line**, it is marked by as many as three small squares, identical to a cursor: one at the midpoint and one at either end point of the selected line segment. If you now select the *Delete* option that line segment disappears and the main menu is restored. If, instead, you select *Move* or *Copy*, the following text appears in the message area:

```
Move to the midpoint or to an end point and press button.
```

If you move the cursor to the midpoint or to an end point, and press a button, the text in the message area changes into:

```
Drag by moving the cursor; then press button.
```

What happens next depends on the latest selected point: if this is the midpoint, moving the cursor will cause the line segment to move in the same way, all the time parallel to the original line segment and not altering in length, as shown in Fig. 5.7. The difference between *Move* and *Copy* is that with *Move* the original line disappears and with *Copy* it remains. If you choose an end point (instead of the midpoint), the other end point remains where it is, so the line to be moved or copied will change in position and possibly in length.

If the selected object is **text**, the message area will display the following line:

```
Move cursor to target location; then press button.
```

In this way you can either move or copy text in a way similar to moving line segments without altering its size or direction.

The *Arc* option enables you to draw not only arcs but also circles and regular polygons. Although HP-GL includes instructions for circles and arcs, program SDRAW does not use these but rather approximates them by a set of line segments. The main reason for this is that WordPerfect 5.0 does not accept HP-GL instructions for circles and arcs. A positive aspect of the chosen method is that you can use the *Arc* option to draw regular polygons. An arc will be drawn on the basis of a given center, a start point, an angle, and a given number n, which indicates how many line segments are to be used to approximate the arc.

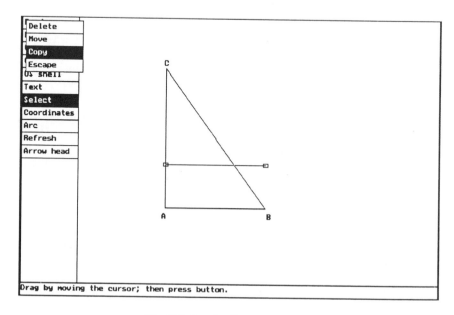

Fig. 5.7. Copying line segment AB

The following requests (for numerical data, in dialog boxes) and messages (in the message area) that successively appear will now be clear:

```
Angle in degrees (negative if clockwise):
How many approximated line segments (e.g. 20):
Press mouse button at center.
Press mouse button at start point.
```

In Fig. 5.4 you can see the first request in a dialog box. After the answer, 360, the request for a number of line segments is displayed. By answering 3, followed by supplying the appropriate center and start points, the triangle shown in Fig. 5.5 can easily be obtained. With complete circles and polygons, that is, with angles of 360°, the orientation (counterclockwise or clockwise) does not make any difference in the result. However, if you want to enter an angle of less than 360°, then a positive number causes the arc to be drawn counter-clockwise; for example, if the given start point lies to the right of the center, the arc is drawn upward. It is drawn clockwise if the angle entered is preceded by a minus sign.

The option *Refresh* first clears the screen and then draws everything again, on the basis of the internal data structure. You will seldom need this option, but if the screen displays any lines or points you don't understand, then you can see whether or not it has really internally been stored in that form by using the *Refresh* option. Normally, the refreshed screen is identical to the original one.

You will sometimes need arrows, the heads of which are drawn by the option *Arrow head*. The heads of arrows in any position can be drawn in a very simple way. When you select the option mentioned, the following message is displayed:

```
Move cursor to arrow tail and press button.
```

As soon as you have done this, the following appears:

```
Move cursor to end of arrow head and press button.
```

Thus, if you want an arrow pointing from A to B, then you first draw line AB in the normal way; after this you can use A (or any point between A and B on that line) as the required 'arrow tail', and you should use B as the 'end of arrow head'. Then a dialog box appears with the following text:

```
Length of arrow head (e.g. 40):
```

Remember that we are using plotter units, hence the rather large suggested value of 40. You can see an example of the arrow heads produced by SDRAW (with arrow length 30) in Fig. 2.8 in Section 2.4.

Programming aspects

SDRAW uses only very simple data structures. There are two tables (with variable names *table* and *strtable*) to store line segments and strings. Although they are used as arrays, these variables are pointers, defined as follows:

```
struct lin_tab_elt {int x1, y1, x2, y2;} *table;
struct str_tab_elt {int x1, y1; char *s;} *strtable;
```

The actual memory space for the 'array elements' is allocated dynamically by means of the function *farmalloc*. As strings have variable length, not the characters themselves but rather a pointer (s) to them is stored in each structure *strtable[i]*. The characters of the strings themselves are stored in dynamically allocated memory. Each time a line or string is entered it is placed at the end or *table* or *strtable*, as the functions *addline* and *addstring* show. When a line or string is deleted, all elements that follow in the table are shifted one position: you can find the program statements

```
table[l] = table[l+1];
strtable[l] = strtable[l+1];
```

for such shifts in the functions *selectlinoptions* and *selecttxtoptions*, respectively.

As you have seen in the section on User aspects, we can temporarily go to DOS, just as we can, for instance, when working with the Turbo C Integrated Environment. (In the latter case you can do this by selecting Alt-F, O.) The way this can be done is extremely simple; for the actual going to DOS and returning to our program, all we have to write is:

```
system("");
```

Normally, the function *system* is used to perform some DOS command, which we supply to this function as a string argument. If this string is empty, we simply go to DOS, with our program remaining in memory. If we type *EXIT*, program execution is resumed after the call to *system*. For our program things are not really as simple as this because we are working in the graphics mode. We must therefore not forget to switch to text mode before we call the *system* function. Analogously, we have to switch to the graphics mode after that call. We then restore the screen on the basis of *table* and *txttable*. The function *refresh* will take care of this; incidentally, this function is also called when the user selects the *Refresh* option of the main menu. Finally, the cursor must be restored; this is done by means of its current coordinates, supplied as arguments. Here is function *os_shell* as it is actually used in SDRAW:

```
void os_shell(int x, int y)
{ to_text(); printf("Type EXIT to return to SDRAW.");
  system("");        /* Go to OS shell */
  initgr(); refresh(x, y);
}
```

Many functions in program SDRAW are similar to those used in the programs
MSDEMO1, MSDEMO2, and MSMENU, discussed in the preceding sections,
so you should refer to those programs if you want to know how SDRAW works
but find some programming details difficult to understand.

```
/* SDRAW: Line drawing, using a mouse and a menu.
*/

#include <conio.h>
#include <dos.h>
#include <stdio.h>
#include <alloc.h>
#include <process.h>
#include <string.h>
#include <ctype.h>
#include <stdlib.h>
#include <math.h>
#include "grasptc.h"

#define LINTABLEN 8000
#define STRTABLEN 1000
#define MENUWIDTH 100
#define BOXH 16
#define ESC 27
union REGS regs;

void circ_arc(int *px, int *py);
int Xpixel(int x), Ypixel(int y), xhpg(int X), yhpg(int Y);
int msinit(int Xlo, int Xhi, int Ylo, int Yhi);
void msget(int *pX, int *pY, int *pbuttons);
int msread(int *pX, int *pY, int *pbuttons);

void cursor(int X, int Y);
void addline(int Xstart, int Ystart, int X, int Y);
void addstring(int X, int Y, char *str);
void wrlines(void);
int confirmed(void);
void rdlines(void);
void initmenu(void);
int getstring(int X, int Y, char *mes, char *str, int boxcode);
void clearrectangle(int Xtop, int Ytop, int Xbottom, int Ybottom);
char ermes(char *str);
```

```
void displaybotlin(char *str);
void defaultbotlin(void);
void drline(int x1, int y1, int x2, int y2);
void drawnewline(int x1, int y1, int x2, int y2);
void endprogram(void);
void newposition(int *px, int *py, int *pX, int *pY, int *pbut);
void refresh(int x, int y);
void textinput(int *px, int *py, int *pX, int *pY);
void selectobject(int *pX, int *pY);
void getline(int *pXstart, int *pYstart);
void txtcursor(int X, int Y);
void selectlinoptions
(int i, int *pX, int *pY, int XX1, int YY1, int XX2, int YY2);
void selecttxtoptions(int i, int *px, int *py);
void secondmenu(void);
void boxes(int n, int primary);
void invertbox(int i, int x, int y, int primary);
void os_shell(int x, int y);
void arrowhead(int *px, int *py);
int round(float x);

struct lin_tab_elt {int x1, y1, x2, y2;} *table;
struct str_tab_elt {int x1, y1; char *s;} *strtable;

int ntable=0, ntxttable=0, Xmin, Ymin, Xmax, Ymax, xmin, ymin,
  xmax, ymax, charheight, charwidth, leftboundary, cursordraw;

char *menuptr, *linbufptr, *boxbuf;
long x_max200, y_max200;
int y200, coordinates=0, modified=0;

#define txt(linenr, str) gotoxy(1, linenr); cprintf(str);

main()
{ int buttons, xm, ym, i, X, Y, x, y;
  clrscr();
  txt(1, "SDRAW: A program to draw lines, arcs, and text, and to produce");
  txt(2, "HP-GL files; these files can be read by this very program and");
  txt(3, "by, for example, WordPerfect 5.0 and Ventura Publisher.");
  txt(5, "You can draw straight lines as follows:");
  txt(6, "Move the cursor to one end point of the line, then press");
  txt(7, "a mouse button, and move the cursor to the other end point.");
  txt(8, "Finally, release the mouse button.");
  txt(10, "Normally, the cursor can be placed only at grid points");
  txt(11, "that horizontally and vertically lie eight units apart.");
  txt(12, "If you want the cursor to move very small distances, use");
  txt(13, "the four arrow keys. Press the Home-key to move the cursor");
  txt(14, "back to the nearest grid point.");
```

```
txt(16, "For other operations, use the mouse and the menu and follow");
txt(17, "the directions displayed on the bottom line.");
txt(19, "Press any key on the keyboard..."); getch();
initgr();
charwidth = textwidth("A"); charheight = textheight("A");
x_max200 = 200 * x_max; y_max200 = y200 = 200 * y_max;
Xmin = 4; Xmax = X__max - 4;
Ymin = 2; Ymax = Y__max - 16;
table = farmalloc((long) LINTABLEN * sizeof(struct lin_tab_elt));
strtable = farmalloc((long) STRTABLEN * sizeof(struct str_tab_elt));
menuptr = farmalloc((long)imagesize(0, 0, MENUWIDTH+1, Ymax-1));
linbufptr = farmalloc((long)imagesize(MENUWIDTH, 0, X__max, 16));
boxbuf = farmalloc((long)imagesize(0, 0, MENUWIDTH-2, BOXH));
if (table == NULL || strtable == NULL || menuptr == NULL ||
    linbufptr == NULL || boxbuf == NULL)
{ to_text(); cprintf("Mem. error"); exit(1);
}
xmax = xhpg(Xmax); ymax = yhpg(Ymin);
xmin = xhpg(Xmin); ymin = yhpg(Ymax);
leftboundary = xhpg(MENUWIDTH+14);


if (msinit(0, (int)x_max200, 0, (int)y_max200) == 0)
{ to_text(); cprintf("No mouse or mouse driver");
  exit(1);
}
while (msread(&xm, &ym, &buttons) >= 0) ;

x = xm; y = ym;
refresh(x, y);
do
{ newposition(&x, &y, &X, &Y, &buttons);
  if (buttons && X < MENUWIDTH)
  { do newposition(&x, &y, &X, &Y, &buttons); while (buttons);
        /* Now the mouse button is no longer pressed down! */
    i = Y/BOXH;
    invertbox(i, x, y, 1); /* Highlight selected item */
    switch (i)
    { case 0: rdlines(); break;
      case 1: wrlines(); break;
      case 2:  /* Clear */
        if (confirmed())
        { ntable = ntxttable = 0; modified = 0; refresh(x, y);
        } else invertbox(i, x, y, 1);
        break;
      case 3: if (confirmed()) endprogram(); break;
      case 4: os_shell(x, y); break;
      case 5:
```

```
        textinput(&x, &y, &X, &Y); break;
      case 6:
        selectobject(&x, &y); break;
      case 7:
        coordinates = 1 - coordinates;
        clearrectangle(512, Ymax+2, Xmax-1, Y__max-1);
        break;
      case 8:
        circ_arc(&x, &y); break;
      case 9:
        refresh(x, y); break;
      case 10: arrowhead(&x, &y);
    }
    if (i != 2 && i != 4 && i != 9) invertbox(i, x, y, 1);
  } else
    if (buttons) getline(&x, &y);
  } while (1);
}


/* Functions in alphabetic order:
*/

void addline(int xstart, int ystart, int x, int y)
{ int aux;
  if (xstart == x && ystart == y) return;
  if (ntable == LINTABLEN)
  { displaybotlin("Line table full."); return;
  }
  if (xstart > x || xstart == x && ystart > y)
  { aux = xstart; xstart = x; x = aux;
    aux = ystart; ystart = y; y = aux;
  }
  table[ntable].x1 = xstart; table[ntable].y1 = ystart;
  table[ntable].x2 = x; table[ntable++].y2 = y;
  modified = 1;
}


void addstring(int x, int y, char *str)
{ char *p;
  if (ntxttable == STRTABLEN)
  { displaybotlin("String table full."); return;
  }
  strtable[ntxttable].x1 = x;
  strtable[ntxttable].y1 = y;
  p = farmalloc((long) (strlen(str)+2));
  if (p == NULL) {to_text(); cprintf("Mem. problem"); exit(1);}
  strcpy(p, str);
  strtable[ntxttable++].s = p;
```

```
    modified = 1;
}


void arrowhead(int *px, int *py)
{ int xhead, yhead, xtail, ytail, X, Y, buttons, xar[3], yar[3], i;
  float phi, len, xx[3], yy[3], c, s;
  char str[50];
  displaybotlin("Move cursor to arrow tail and press button.");
  do newposition(px, py, &X, &Y, &buttons); while (buttons == 0);
  xtail = *px; ytail = *py;
  displaybotlin("Move cursor to end of arrow head and press button.");
  do newposition(px, py, &X, &Y, &buttons); while (buttons == 0);
  xhead = *px; yhead = *py;
  phi = angle(xhead-xtail, yhead-ytail);
  c = cos(phi); s = sin(phi);
  if (getstring(MENUWIDTH+20, 100,
  "Length of arrow head (e.g. 40): ", str, 1) == 0) return;
  if (sscanf(str, "%f", &len) == 0 || len <= 0) return;
  xx[0] = yy[0] = 0.0; xx[1] = xx[2] = -len;
  yy[1] = 0.3 * len; yy[2] = -yy[1];
  xar[0] = xhead; yar[0] = yhead;
  for (i=1; i<3; i++)
  { xar[i] = xhead + round(c * xx[i] - s * yy[i]);
    yar[i] = yhead + round(s * xx[i] + c * yy[i]);
    drawnewline(xar[i-1], yar[i-1], xar[i], yar[i]);
  }
  drawnewline(xar[2], yar[2], xhead, yhead);
}


void boxes(int n, int primary)
{ int i, left, right, offset, level, bottom;
  if (primary)
  { left = 0; offset = 0; bottom = Ymax;
  } else
  { left=7; offset=5; bottom = offset + n * BOXH;
  }
  right = left+MENUWIDTH-1;
  clearrectangle(left+1, offset+1, right-1, bottom-1);
  setwritemode(COPY_PUT);
  for (i=0; i<=n; i++)
  { level = offset+i*BOXH;
    line(left, level, right, level); /* Horizontal lines */
  }
  line(left, offset, left, bottom); /* Vertical lines   */
  line(right, offset, right, bottom);
  setwritemode(XOR_PUT);
}
```

```c
void circ_arc(int *px, int *py)
{ char str[100];
  float phi=0, delta, x1, y1, x2, y2, alpha, r, rx, ry;
  int i, n=1, X, Y, buttons, xC, yC, xA, yA;
  if (getstring(MENUWIDTH+20, 100,
  "Angle in degrees (negative if clockwise): ", str, 1) == 0) return;
  if (sscanf(str, "%f", &phi) == 0) return;
  phi *= PI/180; /* phi now in radians */
  if (getstring(MENUWIDTH+20, 100,
  "How many approximating line segments (e.g. 20): ", str, 1) == 0)
    return;
  if (sscanf(str, "%d", &n) == 0 || n <= 0) return;
  displaybotlin("Press mouse button at center.");
  do newposition(px, py, &X, &Y, &buttons); while (buttons == 0);
  xC = *px; yC = *py; cursor(xC, yC); /* Keep center marked */
  cursordraw = 1 - cursordraw;
  displaybotlin("Press mouse button at start point.");
  do newposition(px, py, &X, &Y, &buttons); while (buttons == 0);
  defaultbotlin();
  cursor(xC, yC); /* Erase cursor at center */
  cursordraw = 1 - cursordraw;
  xA = *px; yA = *py; delta = phi/n;
  x1 = xA; y1 = yA; rx = x1-xC; ry = y1-yC;
  alpha = angle(rx, ry); /* 'angle' is defined in LINDRAW */
  r = sqrt(rx * rx + ry * ry);
  cursor(xA, yA); /* Erase cursor because of the COPY_PUT drawmode */
  setwritemode(COPY_PUT);
  for (i=0; i<n; i++)
  { alpha += delta;
    x2 = xC + r * cos(alpha); y2 = yC + r * sin(alpha);
    drawnewline(x1, y1, x2, y2);
    x1 = x2; y1 = y2;
  }
  setwritemode(XOR_PUT);
  cursor(xA, yA); /* Draw cursor */
}


void clearrectangle(int Xtop, int Ytop, int Xbottom, int Ybottom)
{ struct viewporttype vp;
  getviewsettings(&vp);
  setviewport(Xtop, Ytop, Xbottom, Ybottom, 0);
  clearviewport();
  setviewport(vp.left, vp.top, vp.right, vp.bottom, vp.clip);
}


int confirmed(void)
{ char ch;
  if (ntable + ntxttable > 0 && modified)
```

```c
  { ch = ermes("Save drawing? (Y/N/Esc): "); ch = tolower(ch);
    if (ch == ESC) return 0;
    if (ch == 'y') wrlines();
  }
  return 1;
}


void cursor(int x, int y)
{ int Xm4, Xp4, Ym2, Yp2, Ym1, Yp1, X, Y;
  static char str[50];
  X = Xpixel(x); Y = Ypixel(y);
  Xm4=X-4; Xp4=X+4; Ym2=Y-2; Yp2=Y+2; Ym1=Y-1; Yp1=Y+1;
  line(Xm4, Ym2, Xp4, Ym2); line(Xm4, Yp2, Xp4, Yp2);
  line(Xm4, Ym1, Xm4, Yp1); line(Xp4, Ym1, Xp4, Yp1);
  if (coordinates && cursordraw) /* See explanation below */
  { sprintf(str, "x=%4d y=%4d", x, y);
    clearrectangle(512, Ymax+2, Xmax-1, Y__max-1);
    outtextxy(512, Y__max-5, str);
  }
  cursordraw = 1 -cursordraw;
  /* Values of 'cursordraw': 1, 0, 1, 0, 1, ... */
  /* See also refresh().                       */
}


void defaultbotlin(void)
{ displaybotlin("");
}


void displaybotlin(char *str)
{ clearrectangle(1, Ymax+2, X__max-1, Y__max-1);
  outtextxy(2, Y__max-5, str);
}


void drawnewline(int x1, int y1, int x2, int y2)
{ drline(x1, y1, x2, y2);
  addline(x1, y1, x2, y2);
}


void drline(int x1, int y1, int x2, int y2)
{ int aux, X1, Y1, X2, Y2;
  X1 = Xpixel(x1); Y1 = Ypixel(y1);
  X2 = Xpixel(x2); Y2 = Ypixel(y2);
  if (X1 == X2 && Y1 == Y2) return;
  if (X1 > X2 || X1 == X2 && Y1 > Y2)
  { aux = X1; X1 = X2; X2 = aux;
    aux = Y1; Y1 = Y2; Y2 = aux;
  }
  if (X1 < MENUWIDTH+8) X1 = MENUWIDTH+8;
```

```
   line(X1, Y1, X2, Y2);
}

void endprogram(void)
{ to_text(); exit(0);
}

char ermes(char *str)
{ int left=MENUWIDTH+20;
  char ch;
  getimage(left, 100, Xmax, 116, linbufptr);
  clearrectangle(left, 100, Xmax, 114);
  outtextxy(left+8, 112, str);
  ch = getch();
  putimage(left, 100, linbufptr, COPY_PUT);
  return ch;
}

void getline(int *pxstart, int *pystart)
{ int x, y, xstart, ystart, buttons, x0, y0, X, Y;
  x = xstart = *pxstart; X = Xpixel(x);
  y = ystart = *pystart; Y = Ypixel(y);
  do
  { x0 = x; y0 = y;
    newposition(&x, &y, &X, &Y, &buttons);
    if (x != x0 || y != y0)
    { drline(xstart, ystart, x0, y0);      /* Erase */
      if (x < leftboundary) {*pxstart=x; *pystart=y; return;}
      drline(xstart, ystart, x, y);        /* Drag  */
    }
  } while (buttons);
  addline(xstart, ystart, x, y);
  *pxstart=x; *pystart=y;
}

int getstring(int X, int Y, char *mes, char *str, int boxcode)
{ int len=strlen(mes), i=0, j, maxlen, k;
  char ch, s2[2];
  maxlen=X__max-10-X; s2[1] = '\0';
  if (boxcode)
  { getimage(X, Y-14, X__max-10, Y+2, linbufptr);
    clearrectangle(X, Y-14, X__max-10, Y+2);
    rectangle(X, Y-14, X__max-10, Y+2);
    outtextxy(X+4, Y, mes);
  }
  while(1)
  { j = (len+i)*charwidth;
    if (j >= maxlen) break;
```

```
    txtcursor(X+j, Y-6); /* Draw text cursor */
    ch = getch();
    txtcursor(X+j, Y-6); /* Erase text cursor */
    if (ch == ESC) {i=0; break;}
    if (ch == '\n' || ch == '\r') break;
    if (ch == 8) /* backspace */
    { if (--i < 0) i = 0;
      k = (len+i)*charwidth;
      clearrectangle(X+k, Y-charheight, X+k+charwidth, Y);
    } else
    { str[i] = s2[0] = ch;
      outtextxy(X+j, Y, s2);
      i++;
    }
  }
  str[i] = '\0';
  if (boxcode) putimage(X, Y-14, linbufptr, COPY_PUT);
  return *str;
}

void initmenu(void)
{ int Y=BOXH/2+4;
  boxes(11, 1);
  outtextxy(4, Y, "Read");
  outtextxy(4, Y+=BOXH, "Write");
  outtextxy(4, Y+=BOXH, "Clear");
  outtextxy(4, Y+=BOXH, "Quit");
  outtextxy(4, Y+=BOXH, "OS shell");
  outtextxy(4, Y+=BOXH, "Text");
  outtextxy(4, Y+=BOXH, "Select");
  outtextxy(4, Y+=BOXH, "Coordinates");
  outtextxy(4, Y+=BOXH, "Arc");
  outtextxy(4, Y+=BOXH, "Refresh");
  outtextxy(4, Y+=BOXH, "Arrow head");
}

void invertbox(int i, int x, int y, int primary)
{ int left, right, offset, level; /* See also function 'boxes' */
  if (primary) {left=0; offset=0;} else {left=7; offset=5;}
  right = left+MENUWIDTH-1;
  level = offset + i * BOXH;
  cursor(x, y); /* Erase */
  getimage(left+1, level+1,  right-1, level+BOXH-1, boxbuf);
  putimage(left+1, level+1, boxbuf, NOT_PUT);
  cursor(x, y); /* Restore */
}

int msinit(int Xlo, int Xhi, int Ylo, int Yhi)
```

```
{ int retcode;
  regs.x.ax = 0;
  int86(51, &regs, &regs);
  retcode = regs.x.ax; /* -1: installed; 0: not installed */
  if (retcode == 0) return 0;
  regs.x.ax = 7; regs.x.cx = Xlo; regs.x.dx = Xhi;
  int86(51, &regs, &regs);
  regs.x.ax = 8; regs.x.cx = Ylo; regs.x.dx = Yhi;
  int86(51, &regs, &regs);
  return retcode;
}


int msread(int *px, int *py, int *pbuttons)
{ static int x0=-10000, y0, but0;
  int xnew, ynew;
  do
  { if (kbhit()) return getch(); /* Key input */
    regs.x.ax = 3;
    int86(51, &regs, &regs);
    xnew = regs.x.cx; ynew = regs.x.dx;
    *pbuttons = regs.x.bx;
  } while (xnew == x0 && ynew == y0 && *pbuttons == but0);
  *px = xnew; *py = y200 - ynew;
  x0 = xnew; y0 = ynew; but0 = *pbuttons;
  return -1;                    /* -1: No key input */
}


void newposition(int *px, int *py, int *pX, int *pY, int *pbut)
{ int ch, x0=*px, y0=*py, x, y;
  static int xm, ym, xcorr=0, ycorr=0;
  ch = msread(&xm, &ym, pbut); ch = tolower(ch);
  if (ch >= 0)
  { if (ch == 0)   /* Arrow keys are read as two characters, */
    { ch = getch(); /* the first of which is '\0'.            */
      switch (ch)
      { case 72: ycorr++; break;            /* Up    */
        case 75: xcorr--; break;            /* Left  */
        case 77: xcorr++; break;            /* Right */
        case 80: ycorr--; break;            /* Down  */
        case 71: xcorr = ycorr = 0; break; /* Home   */
      }
    }
  }
  x = xm + xcorr; y = ym + ycorr;
  if (x < xmin) x = xmin;
  if (x > xmax) x = xmax;
  if (y < ymin) y = ymin;
  if (y > ymax) y = ymax;
```

```c
  if (x != x0 || y != y0)
  { cursor(x0, y0);     /* Erase   */
    cursor(x, y);       /* Display */
  }
  *px = x; *py = y;
  *pX = Xpixel(x); *pY = Ypixel(y);
}

void os_shell(int x, int y)
{ to_text(); printf("Type EXIT to return to SDRAW.");
  system("");          /* Go to OS shell */
  initgr(); refresh(x, y);
}

void rdlines(void)
{ FILE *fp;
  int x1, y1, x2, y2, i, freshstart;
  char str[100], ch;
  if (getstring(MENUWIDTH+4, 18, "File name: ", str, 1) == 0) return;
  fp = fopen(str, "r");
  if (fp == NULL)
  { while (ermes("Can't open file; press Esc.") != ESC) ;
    return;
  }
  freshstart = (ntable + ntxttable == 0);
  do ch = getc(fp); while (ch != '\n' && ch != EOF);
  setwritemode(COPY_PUT);
  while (fscanf(fp, "LT;PU;PA%d,%d;PD;PA%d,%d;",
                     &x1, &y1, &x2, &y2) == 4)
  { drawnewline(x1, y1, x2, y2);
    while (getc(fp) != '\n') ; /* Skip rest of input line */
  }
  setwritemode(XOR_PUT);
  while (fscanf(fp, "PU;PA%d,%d;LB", &x1, &y1) == 2)
  { i = 0;
    while (ch = getc(fp), ch != '\003' && ch != EOF) str[i++] = ch;
    str[i] = '\0';
    do ch = getc(fp); while (ch != '\n');
    addstring(x1, y1, str);
    outtextxy(Xpixel(x1), Ypixel(y1), str);
  }
  fclose(fp);
  if (freshstart) modified = 0;
}

void refresh(int x, int y)
{ int i;
  static first=1;
```

```
    settextjustify(LEFT_TEXT, BOTTOM_TEXT); /* HP-GL convention */
    if (first) first=0;/* Saves time */ else clearviewport();
    rectangle(0, 0, X__max, Y__max);
    line(0, Ymax, X__max, Ymax);
    defaultbotlin();
    initmenu();
    setwritemode(COPY_PUT);
    for (i=0; i<ntable; i++)
      drline(table[i].x1, table[i].y1, table[i].x2, table[i].y2);
    for (i=0; i<ntxttable; i++)
      outtextxy(Xpixel(strtable[i].x1),Ypixel(strtable[i].y1),strtable[i].s);
    setwritemode(XOR_PUT);
    cursordraw = 1;   /* If cursordraw = 1, cursor() draws a new cursor; */
    cursor(x, y);     /* if cursordraw = 0, cursor() erases the old one. */
}


int round(float x)
{ return (int)(x < 0 ? x - 0.5 : x + 0.5);
}


void secondmenu(void)
{ int Y=BOXH/2+9;
  getimage(0, 0, MENUWIDTH+8, Ymax-1, menuptr);
  boxes(4, 0);
  outtextxy(12, Y, "Delete");
  outtextxy(12, Y+=BOXH, "Move");
  outtextxy(12, Y+=BOXH, "Copy");
  outtextxy(12, Y+=BOXH, "Escape");
  displaybotlin("Select operation.");
}


void selectlinoptions
(int i, int *px, int *py, int xx1, int yy1, int xx2, int yy2)
{ int j, l, x=*px, y=*py, x0, y0, dragmode, xxm, yym, buttons,
      *pivotx, *pivoty, dx, dy, first=1, X, Y, XXm, YYm,
      XX1=Xpixel(xx1), YY1=Ypixel(yy1), XX2=Xpixel(xx2), YY2=Ypixel(yy2);
  cursor(xx1, yy1); cursor(xx2, yy2); /* Display cursors at end points */
  xxm = (xx1+xx2)/2; yym = (yy1 + yy2)/2;
  XXm = Xpixel(xxm); YYm = Ypixel(yym);
  cursor(xxm, yym);      /* Display cursor at midpoint */
  cursor(x, y);          /* Erase                     */
  secondmenu();          /* Display secondary menu    */
  cursor(x, y);          /* Restore                   */
  do
  { newposition(&x, &y, &X, &Y, &buttons);
  } while (buttons == 0 || X >= MENUWIDTH || Y >= 5+4*BOXH);
  j = (Y-5)/BOXH;
  invertbox(j, x, y, 0);
```

```
switch(j)
{ case 0: /* Delete */
  { ntable--;
    for (l=i; l<ntable; l++) table[l] = table[l+1];
    drline(xx1, yy1, xx2, yy2); /* Erase */
    break;
  }
  case 1: case 2: /* Move or Copy, respectively */
  { displaybotlin(
    "Move to the midpoint or to an end point and press button.");
    dragmode = -1;
    do
    { newposition(&x, &y, &X, &Y, &buttons);
      if (abs(X-XX1) < 3 && abs(Y-YY1) < 3) dragmode = 1; else
      if (abs(X-XX2) < 3 && abs(Y-YY2) < 3) dragmode = 2; else
      if (abs(X-XXm) < 9 && abs(Y-YYm) < 9) dragmode = 0;
    } while (buttons == 0 || dragmode < 0);
    while (newposition(&x, &y, &X, &Y, &buttons), buttons) ;
    /* Now buttons == 0 */
    x0 = x; y0 = y;
    displaybotlin("Drag by moving the cursor; then press button.");
    while (newposition(&x, &y, &X, &Y, &buttons), buttons==0)
    { if (dragmode == 0) {pivotx = &xxm; pivoty = &yym;} else
      if (dragmode == 1) {pivotx = &xx1; pivoty = &yy1;} else
                         {pivotx = &xx2; pivoty = &yy2;}
      if (x != *pivotx || y != *pivoty)
      { if (j == 1 || !first) drline(xx1, yy1, xx2, yy2); /* Erase */
        else                              /* 1 = Move,   2 = Copy */
        addline(xx1, yy1, xx2, yy2); /* j = 2: Copy, first time */
        first = 0;
        cursor(xx1, yy1); cursor(xx2, yy2); cursor(xxm, yym);
        dx = x - x0; dy = y - y0;
        if (dragmode != 2) {xx1 += dx; yy1 += dy;} /* 0 or 1 */
        if (dragmode != 1) {xx2 += dx; yy2 += dy;} /* 0 or 1 */
        xxm = (xx1+xx2)/2; yym = (yy1 + yy2)/2;
        x0 = x; y0 = y;
        drline(xx1, yy1, xx2, yy2);
        cursor(xx1, yy1); cursor(xx2, yy2); cursor(xxm, yym);
        table[i].x1 = xx1; table[i].y1 = yy1;
        table[i].x2 = xx2; table[i].y2 = yy2;
      }
    }
  }
  invertbox(j, x, y, 0);
}
cursor(xx1, yy1); cursor(xx2, yy2); cursor(xxm, yym);
/* Erase cursors at end points and at midpoint */
*px=x; *py=y; defaultbotlin();
```

```
    modified = 1;
  }


  void selectobject(int *px, int *py)
  { int x=*px, y=*py, buttons, i, xx1, yy1, xx2, yy2, dx, dy, X, Y, found=0;
    long deviation;
    displaybotlin("Move cursor to selected object and press button.");
    do newposition(&x, &y, &X, &Y, &buttons); while (buttons == 0);
    defaultbotlin();
    for (i=0; i<ntable && !found; i++)
    { xx1 = table[i].x1; yy1 = table[i].y1;
      xx2 = table[i].x2; yy2 = table[i].y2;
      if (x < xx1-4 || x > xx2+4   /* xx1 <= xx2 */
      || y < yy1-4 && y < yy2 || y > yy1+4 && y > yy2+4) continue;
      dx = xx2 - xx1; dy = yy2 - yy1;
      deviation = (long)(x-xx1)*dy-(long)(y-yy1)*dx;
      if (labs(deviation) < 10*(dx + abs(dy)))
      { selectlinoptions(i, &x, &y, xx1, yy1, xx2, yy2);
        found = 1;
      }
    }
    if (!found)
    { for (i=0; i<ntxttable && !found; i++)
      { xx1 = strtable[i].x1; yy1 = strtable[i].y1;
        if (abs(x-xx1)+abs(y-yy1) < 50)
        { selecttxtoptions(i, &x, &y);
          defaultbotlin();
          found = 1;
        }
      }
    }
    if (!found)
    { displaybotlin("Not found. Press Esc.");
      while (getch() != ESC) ;
      defaultbotlin();
    }
    *px=x; *py=y;
    cursor(x, y); /* Erase */
    putimage(0, 0, menuptr, COPY_PUT);
    cursor(x, y); /* Restore */
  }


  void selecttxtoptions(int i, int *px, int *py)
  { int x=*px, y=*py, j, l;
    char *p=strtable[i].s;
    int xx=strtable[i].x1, yy=strtable[i].y1, X, Y, buttons;
    cursor(x, y);      /* Erase        */
    cursor(xx, yy);    /* Mark string  */
```

```
secondmenu();      /* Secondary menu */
cursor(xx, yy);    /* Unmark string  */
cursor(x, y);      /* Restore        */
do
{ newposition(&x, &y, &X, &Y, &buttons);
} while (buttons == 0 || X>MENUWIDTH+8 || Y>=4*BOXH);
defaultbotlin();
j = Y/BOXH; invertbox(j, x, y, 0);
switch(j)
{ case 0: /* Delete */
    ntxttable--;
    for (l=i; l<ntxttable; l++) strtable[l] = strtable[l+1];
    refresh(x, y); break;
  case 1: case 2: /* Move or Copy, respectively */
    displaybotlin("Move cursor to target location; then press button.");
    while (newposition(&x, &y, &X, &Y, &buttons), buttons==0);
    /* Now button is pressed: arrived at target location */
    while (newposition(&x, &y, &X, &Y, &buttons), buttons);
    /* Button released */
    if (j == 1) /* Move */
    { strtable[i].x1 = x; strtable[i].y1 = y;
    } else addstring(x, y, p);
    refresh(x, y);
  }
  *px = x; *py = y;
  modified = 1;
}


void textinput(int *px, int *py, int *pX, int *pY)
{ int x=*px, y=*py, buttons, X, Y, nonempty;
  char str[100];
  displaybotlin("Move cursor to where text is to begin and press button.");
  do newposition(&x, &y, &X, &Y, &buttons); while (buttons == 0);
  clearrectangle(1, Ymax+2, X__max-1, Y__max-1);
  displaybotlin(
  "Enter text; then press the Enter-key.");
  cursor(x, y); /* Erase */
  nonempty = getstring(Xpixel(x), Ypixel(y), "", str, 0);
  cursor(x, y); /* Restore */
  if (nonempty) addstring(x, y, str);
  defaultbotlin();
  *px=x; *py=y;
  *pX=X; *pY=Y;
}


void txtcursor(int X, int Y)
{ line(X, Y-2, X, Y+2);
  line(X-2, Y-4, X-1, Y-3); line(X+2, Y-4, X+1, Y-3);
```

```
      line(X-2, Y+4, X-1, Y+3); line(X+2, Y+4, X+1, Y+3);
   }

   void wrlines(void)
   { FILE *fp;
     char ch;
     int i, len;
     char str[100];
     if (getstring(104, 30, "File name: ", str, 1) == 0) return;
     fp = fopen(str, "r");
     if (fp != NULL)
     { fclose(fp);
       do
        { ch = ermes("Overwrite existing file? (Y/N): ");
          ch = tolower(ch);
        } while (ch != 'y' && ch != 'n');
        if (ch == 'n') return;
     }
     fp = fopen(str, "w");
     if (fp == NULL)
     { while (ermes("Can't open file; press Esc.") != ESC) ;
       return;
     }
     fprintf(fp, "IN;SC%d,%d,%d,%d;SR1.2,3.0;\n",
                  leftboundary, xmax, ymin, ymax);
     /* HP-GL: Initialize; extreme values of coordinates.
     */
     for (i=0; i<ntable; i++) fprintf(fp, "LT;PU;PA%d,%d;PD;PA%d,%d;\n",
        table[i].x1, table[i].y1, table[i].x2, table[i].y2);
     for (i=0; i<ntxttable; i++)
     { len = strlen(strtable[i].s);
       strtable[i].s[len] = '\003'; strtable[i].s[len+1] = '\0';
       fprintf(fp, "PU;PA%d,%d;LB%s;\n",
         strtable[i].x1, strtable[i].y1, strtable[i].s);
       strtable[i].s[len] = '\0';
     }
     fclose(fp); modified = 0;
   }

   int xhpg(int X)
   { return (int)(X * x_max200 / X__max);
   }

   int Xpixel(int x)
   { return (int)((long)X__max * x / x_max200);
   }

   int yhpg(int Y)
```

```
{ return (int)((Y__max - Y) * y_max200 / Y__max);
}

int Ypixel(int y)
{ return Y__max - (int)((long)Y__max * y / y_max200);
}
```

Bibliography

Ammeraal, L. (1986). *Programming Principles in Computer Graphics*, Chichester: John Wiley.

Ammeraal, L. (1986). *C for Programmers*, Chichester: John Wiley.

Ammeraal, L. (1987). *Computer Graphics for the IBM PC*, Chichester: John Wiley.

Ammeraal, L. (1987). *Programs and Data Structures in C*, Chichester: John Wiley.

Ammeraal, L. (1988). *Interactive 3D Computer Graphics*, Chichester: John Wiley.

Borland International (1988). *Turbo C User's Guide, Turbo C Reference Guide Version 2.0.*

Dettmann, T. R. (1988). *DOS Programmers Reference*, Carmel, Indiana: Que.

Kreyszig, E. (1962). *Advanced Engineering Mathematics*, New York: John Wiley.

Lauwerier, H. A. (1987). *Fractals - Meetkundige Figuren in Eindeloze Herhaling*, Amsterdam: Aramith.

Mosich, D., N. Shammas, and B. Flamig (1988). *Advanced Turbo C Programmer's Guide*, New York: John Wiley.

Norton, P. (1985). *Programmer's Guide to the IBM PC*, Washington: Microsoft Press.

Index

By the Same Author

INTERACTIVE 3D COMPUTER GRAPHICS
0 471 92014 2, 1988, 254pp, Paper

COMPUTER GRAPHICS FOR THE IBM PC
".. a firmly practical book that describes a working graphics environment for this popular microcomputer..", Times Higher Education Supplement

0 471 91501 7, 1987, 141pp, Paper

PROGRAMMING PRINCIPLES IN COMPUTER GRAPHICS
"The approach of this text is far superior to that of most microcomputer graphics...

...The book is among the best starting points I've seen for people who need to learn computer graphics, be they students, teachers, or programmers". BYTE Magazine.

0 471 90989 0, 1986, 168pp, Paper

PROGRAMS AND DATA STRUCTURES IN C
0 471 91751 6, 1987, 206pp, Paper

C FOR PROGRAMMERS
0 471 91128 3, 1986, 176pp, Paper